HELPFUL HEURISTICS HANDBOOK

View Legal

MATTHEW BURGESS AND DYAN BURGESS

 A catalogue record for this book is available from the National Library of Australia

National Library of Australia Cataloguing-in-Publication entry

Creators: Burgess, Matthew, and Burgess, Dyan, authors.

Title: Helpful Heuristics Handbook / Matthew Burgess and Dyan Burgess; book designed by Peggy Rupp Design.

ISBN: 978-1-925406-47-4

Subjects: Burgess, Matthew.
  View Legal (Firm)
  Legal services--Australia.
  Finance, Personal--Australia.
  Assets (Accounting)--Australia.
  Tax planning--Australia.
  Estate planning--Australia.

Other Creators/Contributors: Peggy Rupp Design, book designer.

Helpful Heuristics Handbook
Copyright 2020 Matthew Burgess and Dyan Burgess

The moral right of the authors have been asserted.

Without limiting the rights under copyright reserved above, no part of this publication may be reproduced, stored, or transmitted in any form or by any means, without prior written permission of both the copyright owners and the below publisher of this book.

While the authors have made every effort to provide accurate information at the time of publication, neither the publisher nor the authors assume any responsibility for errors, or for changes that occur after publication. Further the publisher does not have any control over and does not assume any responsibility for third-party content changes.

The information in this book is of a general nature, not intended to be specific professional advice. Please seek the opinion of a professional to advise you for your situation. The authors' opinions are his and her own and do not represent the view of any other person, firm or entity. Edited by the eldest child, Stephanie Burgess, with plenty of guidance from Jasmin, Lily and Aven. All errors that remain are that of said child and the parents take no responsibility.

Published by D & M Fancy Pastry in 2020
Book Design by Peggy Rupp Design
Typefaces ElectraLTStd

"PREDICTIONS ARE TRICKY, PARTICULARLY ABOUT THE FUTURE"

YOGI BERRA

Contents

About this Book ix

Chapter 1: Health 1
Chapter 2: Mentoring 23
Chapter 3: Habits 45
Chapter 4: Thinking 67
Chapter 5: Relationships 89
Chapter 6: Learning 111
Chapter 7: Principles 133
Chapter 8: Tech 155
Chapter 9: Frameworks 177
Chapter 10: Tips 199

Idea Initiators 222
Acknowledgements 230
Interested to learn more? 231
A Selection of Other Books from View Legal 234
About View 236
About the Authors 237
Behind the Scenes 239

About this Book

As set out in the foreword's in other publications in Matthew's Dream Enabler' series, for as long as we can remember, the obsessive study of great thinkers has been our favourite pastime.

One aspect of this has been our evolving approach to 'common placing' – that is, the constant collection and ordering of the ideas of others.

Common placing has evolved, for us, from simply hoarding as many of our favourite books as possible, to cataloguing separately the key extracts, re-cataloguing extracts into disciplines and themes and then to summarising the extracts into a centralised, personal 'bible' loosely titled 'brain food'.

This release, the 'Helpful Heuristics Handbook' sets out some of the content that indirectly inspired us to create other books in The Dream Enabler series.

More broadly the heuristics featured here have also had an evolving and increasingly important place in our day to day thinking and decision making.

As heuristics are designed to be 'rules of thumb' or short cuts to making reliably useful decisions quickly – without any focus on the underlying science; this handbook adopts the same approach.

In relation to any heuristics in this handbook that are not self-explanatory – or indeed that you would like more information or context about – please contact us.

The other alternative of course is to investigate yourself via that ubiquitous heuristic tool (not actually otherwise mentioned in this book); namely leveraging Dr Google.

Or as we were gently reminded recently: 'LMGTFY' is a thing; acknowledging the irony that you may need to Google this...

Health

1. No technology within the last 60 minutes of each day.

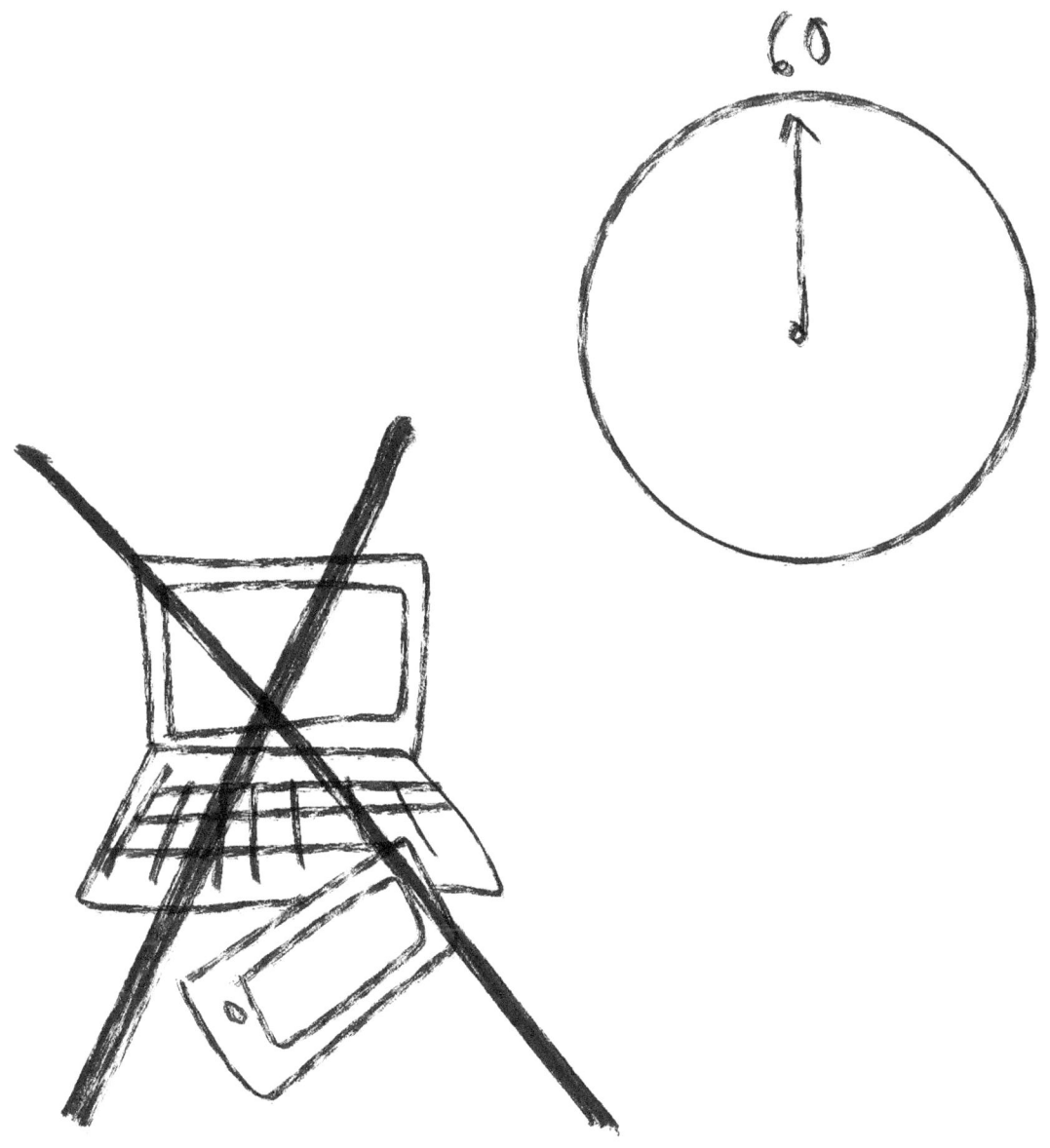

2. Do not use an alarm to wake up unless you absolutely have to.

[#Get the alarm clock that shreds $50 notes every 2 minutes once it goes off.]

3. **Travel the night before; be where you need to be and ready.**

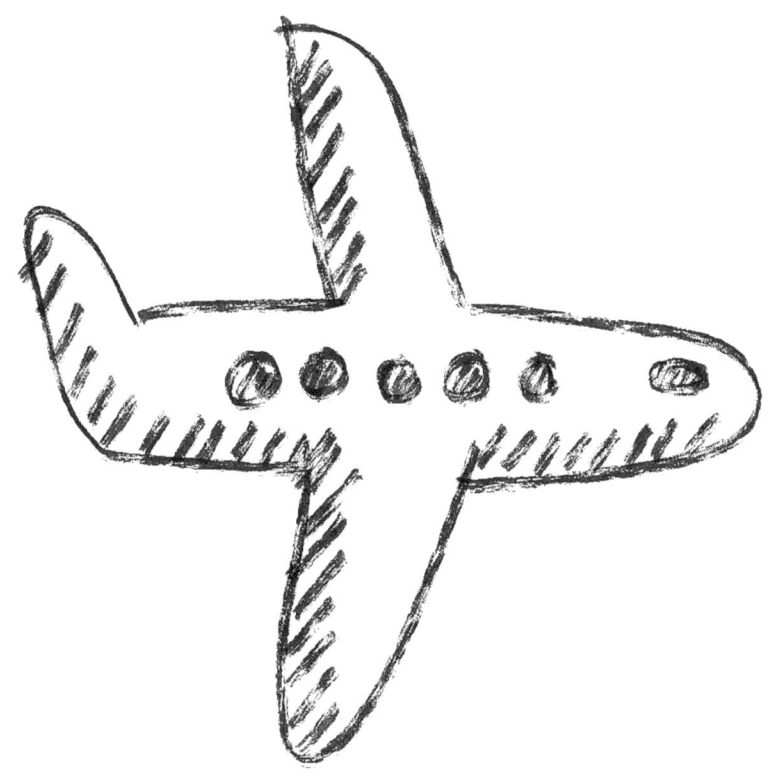

4. **Sleep. 8. Hours.**

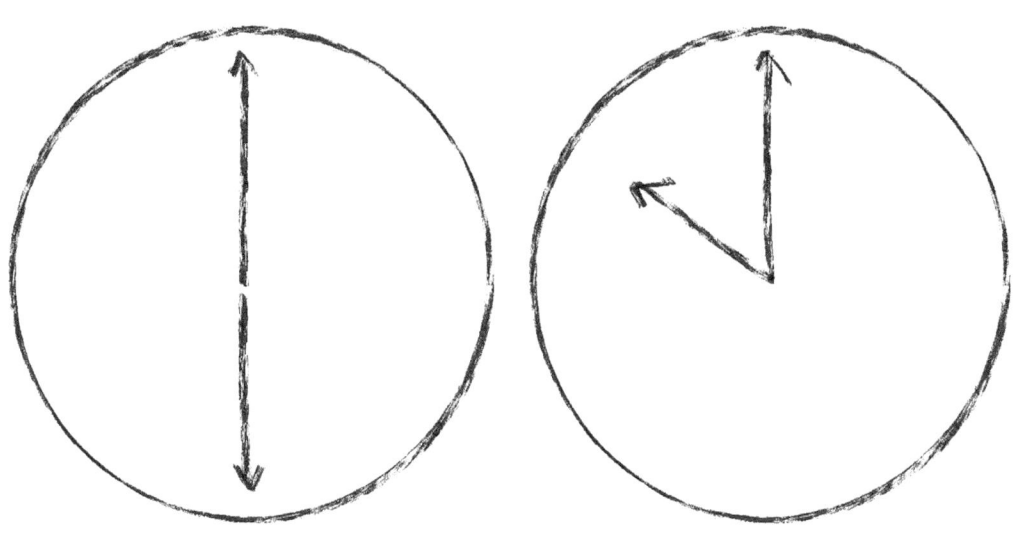

5. Green smoothies.

6. **Great shoes and a great bed.**

[#or great shoes and a good looking spouse.]

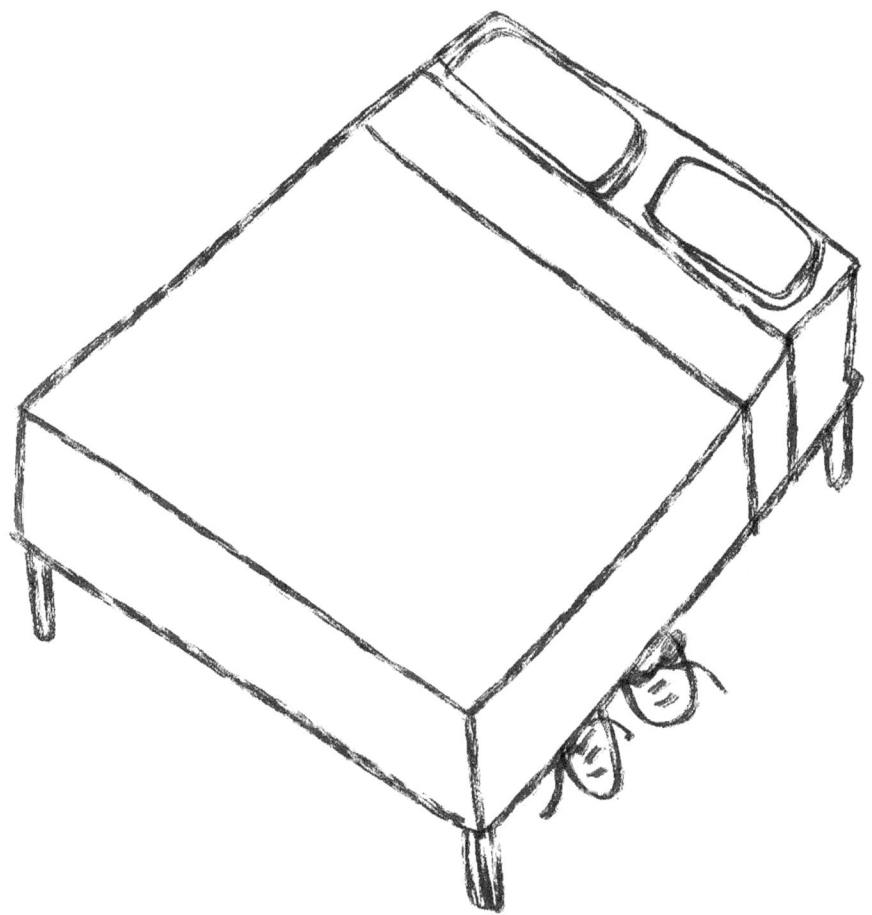

7. Walking adventures.

8. **Breathe. Through. Your. Nose.**

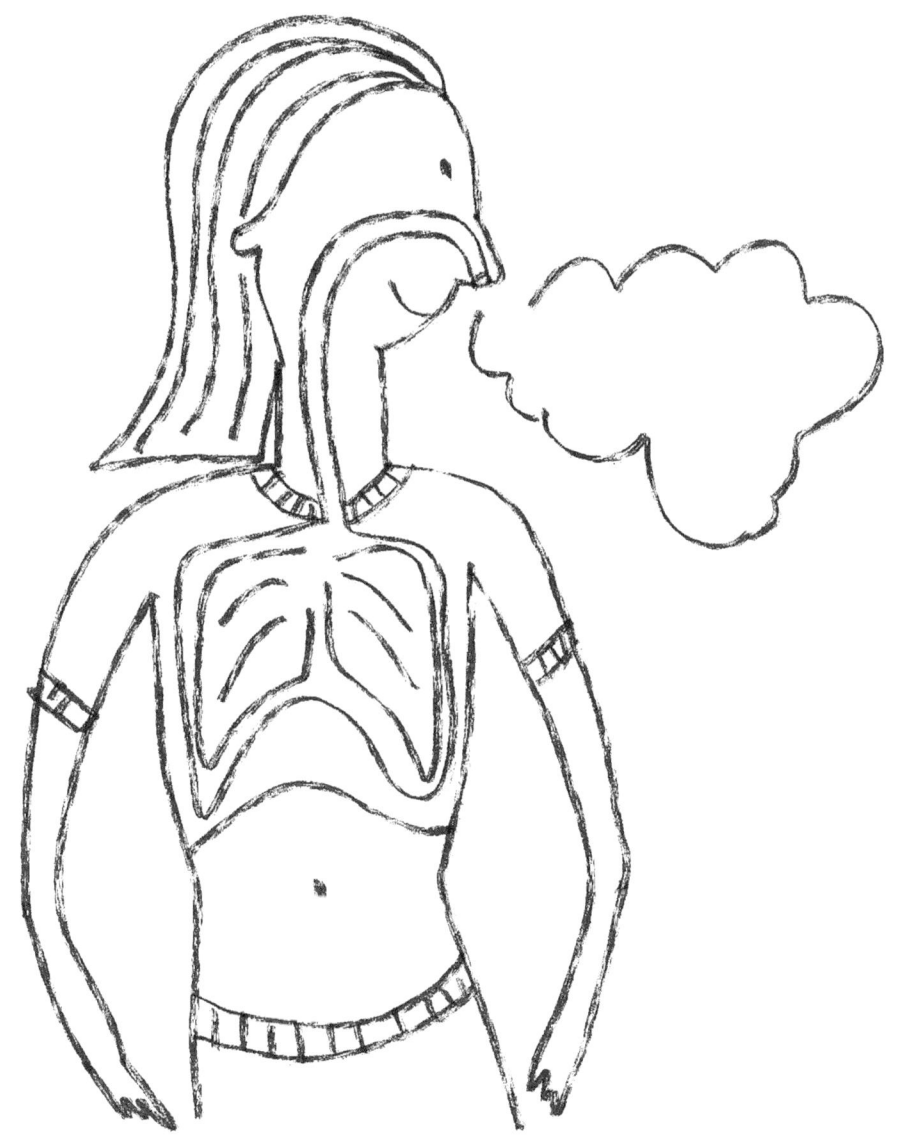

9. **Early to bed, early to rise, work hard and exercise.**

10. Find ways to have regular breaks and ideally leverage them into where you otherwise want to be.

Mentoring

1. **Develop and foster at least one mastermind group in real life and another mastermind group in your dreams.**

2. Share a meal with your family and loved ones at least once a day, around a table; sans devices.

3. Proactively have guests to your family dinner.

4. Actively look for coaches and mentors in books and in your tribe.

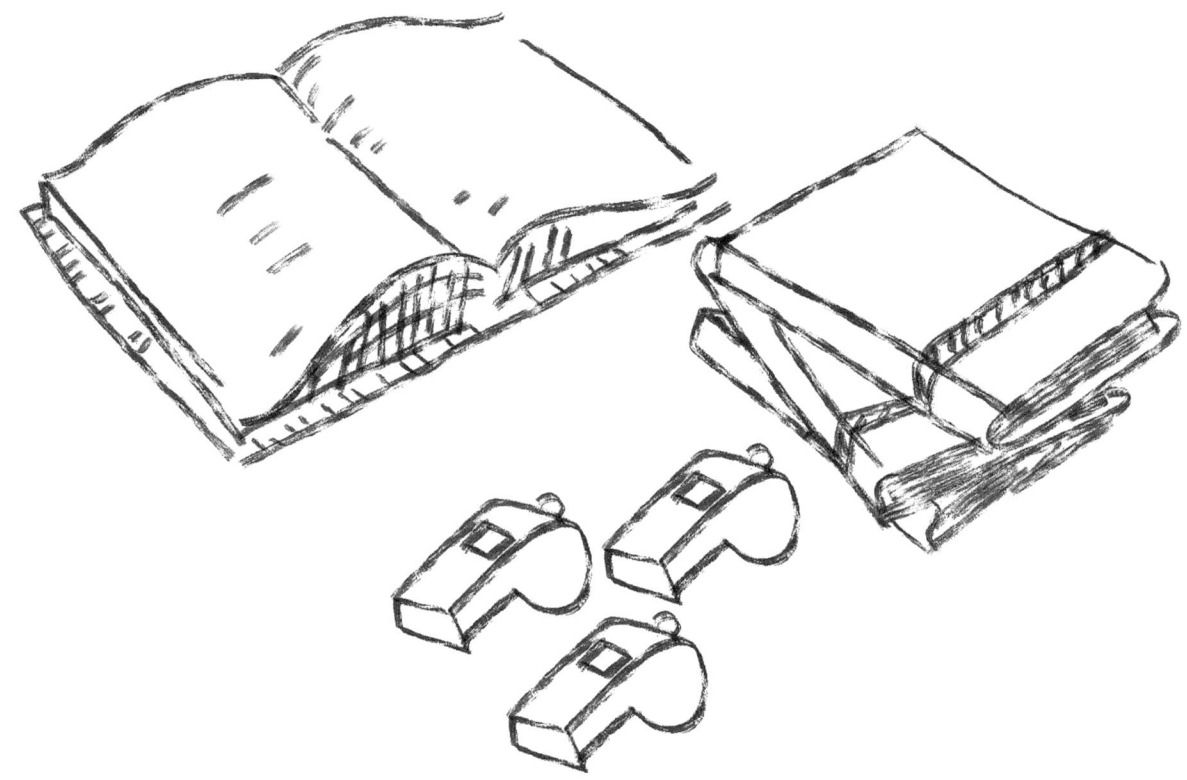

5. Pay it forward.

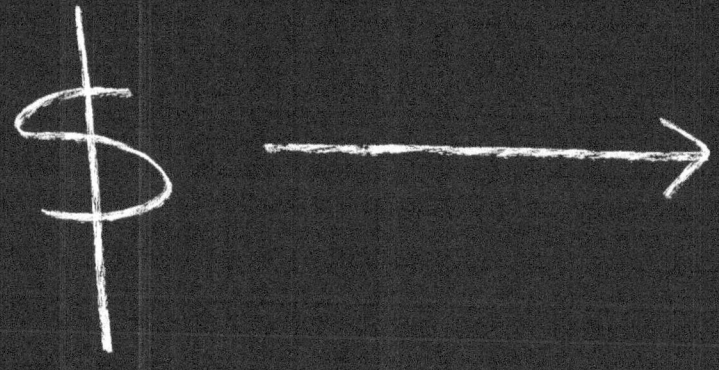

6. Have heroes.

7. Reverse mentoring – the younger they are the less information they have to remove before learning.

8. **The only measure you need for your life: the impact you have on others.**

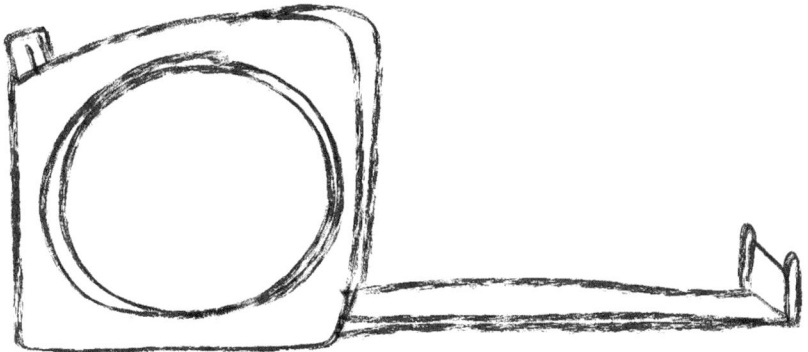

9. Fitzgerald's Intelligence Test: the ability to hold two opposed ideas in mind at the same time and still retain the ability to function.

10. Quality time is accessed only via quantity time.

Habits

1. Meditation and focused thinking.

2. **Embrace start times at, for example, 10 minutes past the hour.**

3. **Multi leverage – for example swimming and meditation.**

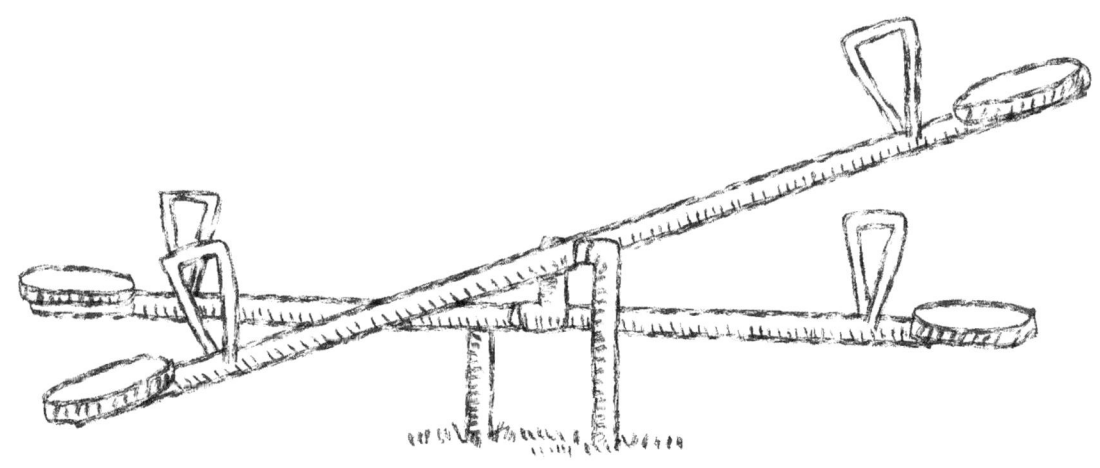

4. **Understand multitasking is only possible with one focused activity, however, look for ways to leverage this – for example doing conference calls while walking.**

[#as opposed to sitting on the toilet while on a conference call.]

5. **Find exercise routines that are unbreakable – for example, do not rely on third parties or external equipment – planking is a great example.**

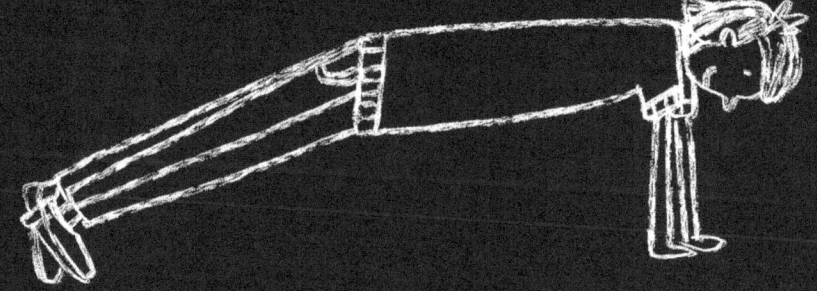

6. **Do the easy things; and your life will be hard.**

7. Embrace storytelling.

8. Bucket list.

9. Live like a Stoic for a week.

10. Have perfect posture and vocal strength.

Thinking

1. **Batch all work. Small tasks can be bundled up. Large tasks should be chunked down.**

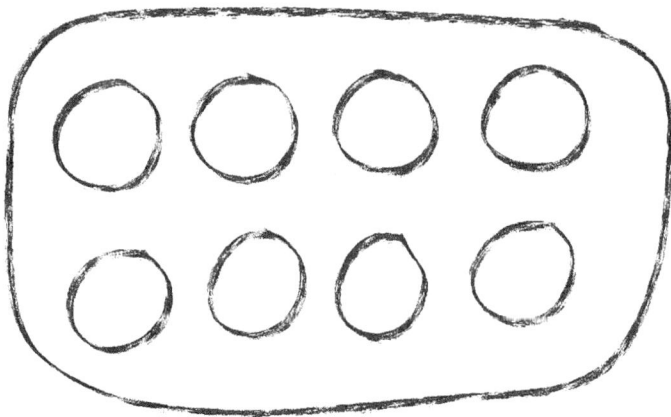

2. Understand the distinction between holidays and travel.

3. Understand the power of and (not or) – in particular, loose and tight.

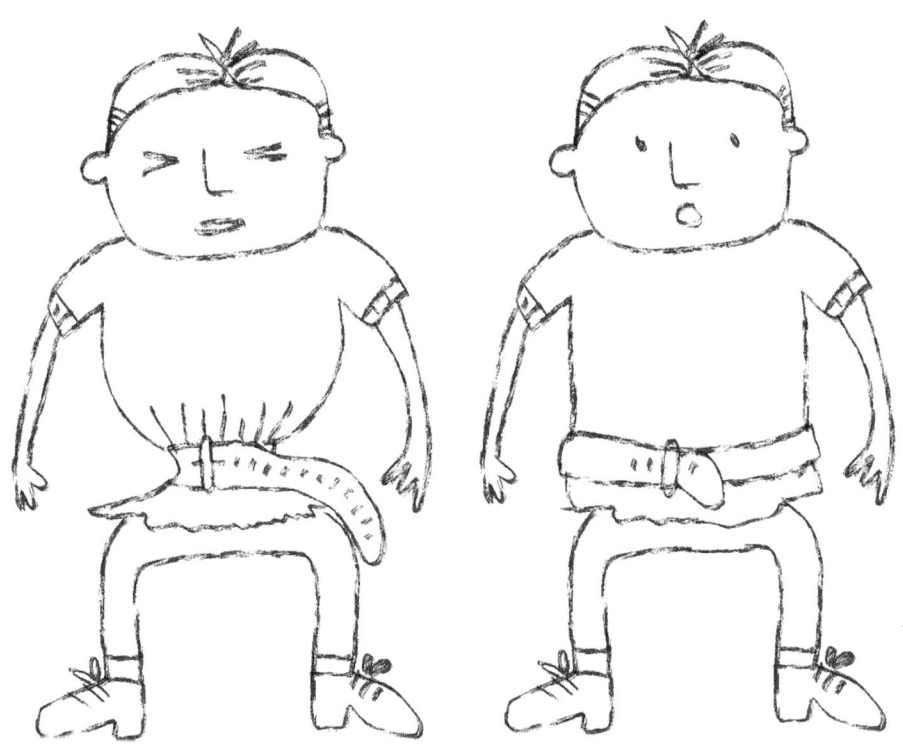

4. Questions; not answers are the key. Michael Bungay Stanier's seven coaching questions:

a. Kickstart Question – What's on your mind?
b. AWE Question – And What Else?
c. Focus Question – What's the real challenge here for you?
d. Foundation Question – What do you want?
e. Lazy Question – How can I help?
f. Strategic Question – If you're saying yes to this, what are you saying no to?
g. Learning Question – What was most useful to you about this conversation?

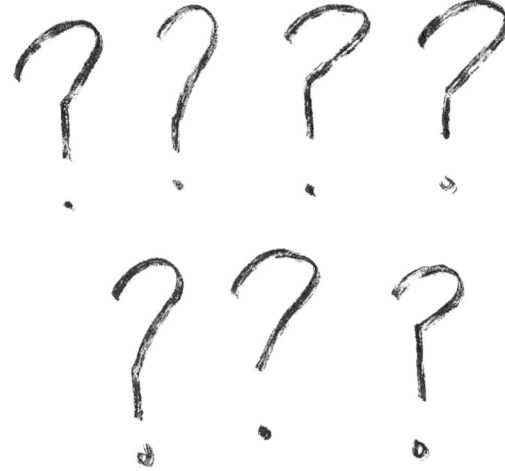

Nathaniel Branden's six pillars of self-esteem:

a. Be conscious, listen deeply, be present (an un-anxious presence)
b. Self-acceptance – including accepting feelings and thinking about them
c. Self-responsibility – autonomy, freedom and accountability – they are all the same thing
d. Self-assertiveness – respecting your rights and the rights of others and be halfway between passive and aggressive
e. Living purposefully – starting with why
f. Personal integrity – your character is your destiny

6. Maria Popova's ten learnings:

a. Allow yourself the uncomfortable luxury of changing your mind
b. Do nothing for prestige or status or money or approval alone (or as Munger once said: 'Would you rather be the world's greatest lover, but have everyone think you're the world's worst lover? Or would you rather be the world's worst lover but have everyone think you're the world's greatest lover?')
c. Be generous
d. Build pockets of stillness into your life
e. When people tell you who they are, believe them. When people try to tell you who you are, don't believe them
f. Presence is far more intricate and rewarding an art than productivity
g. Expect anything worthwhile to take a long time
h. Seek out what magnifies your spirit
i. Embrace being an idealist
j. Fight cynicism

7. Embrace the eighth wonder of the world – compounding.

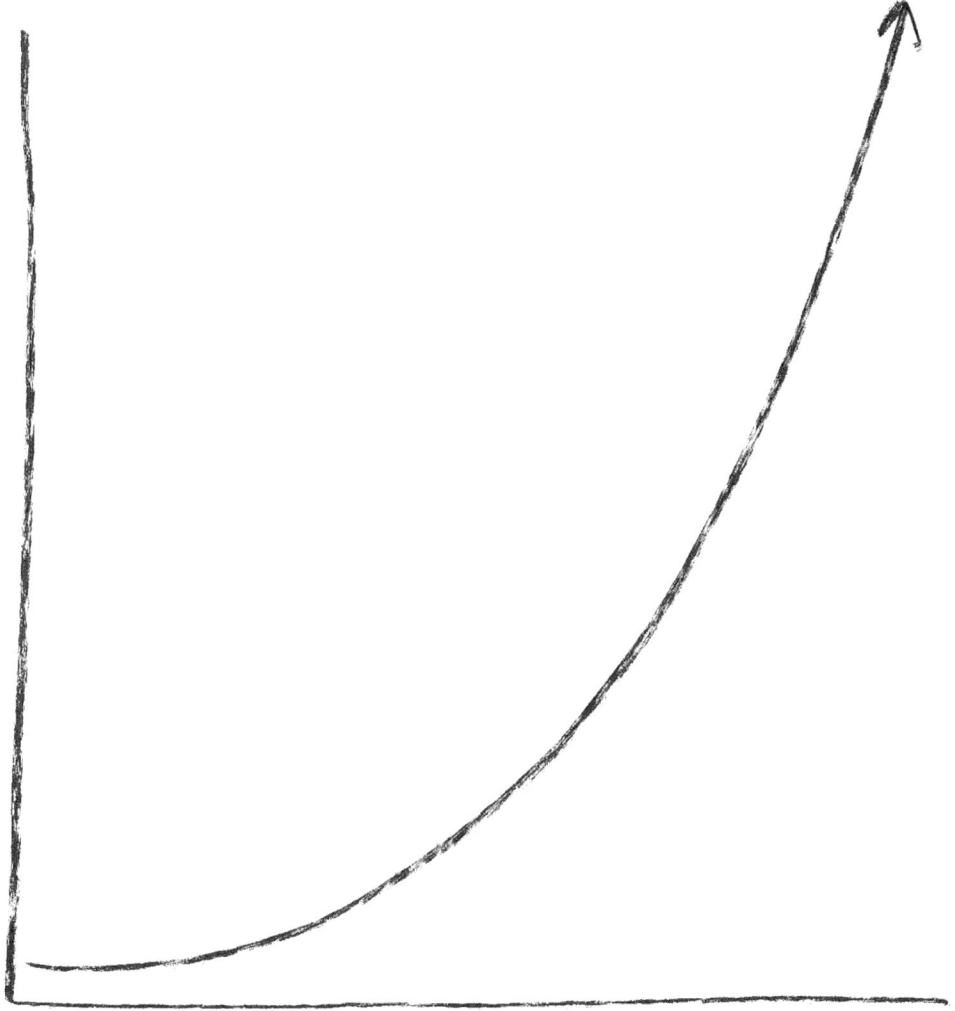

8. **Allow serendipity to occur.**

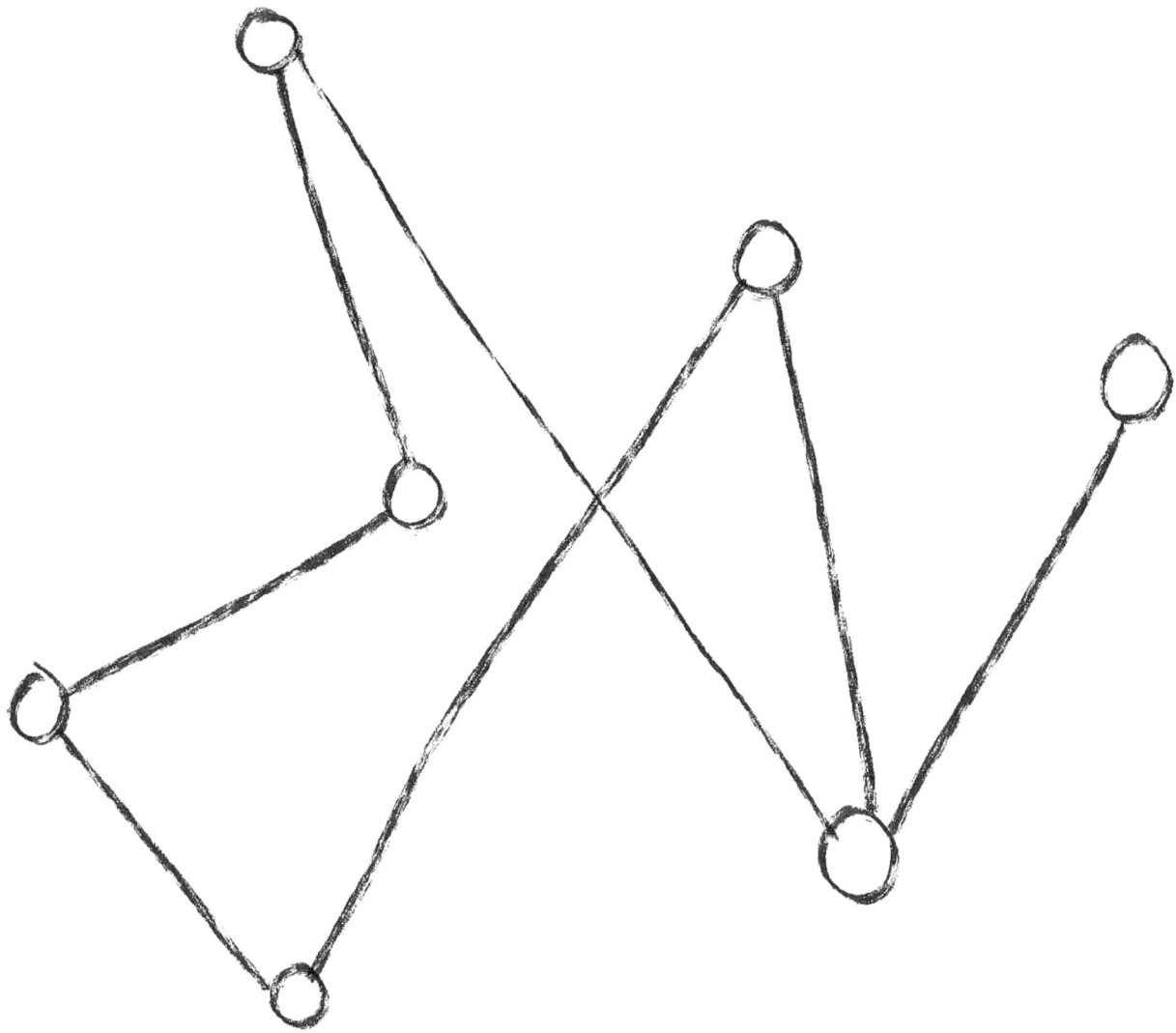

9. Foster synchronicity.

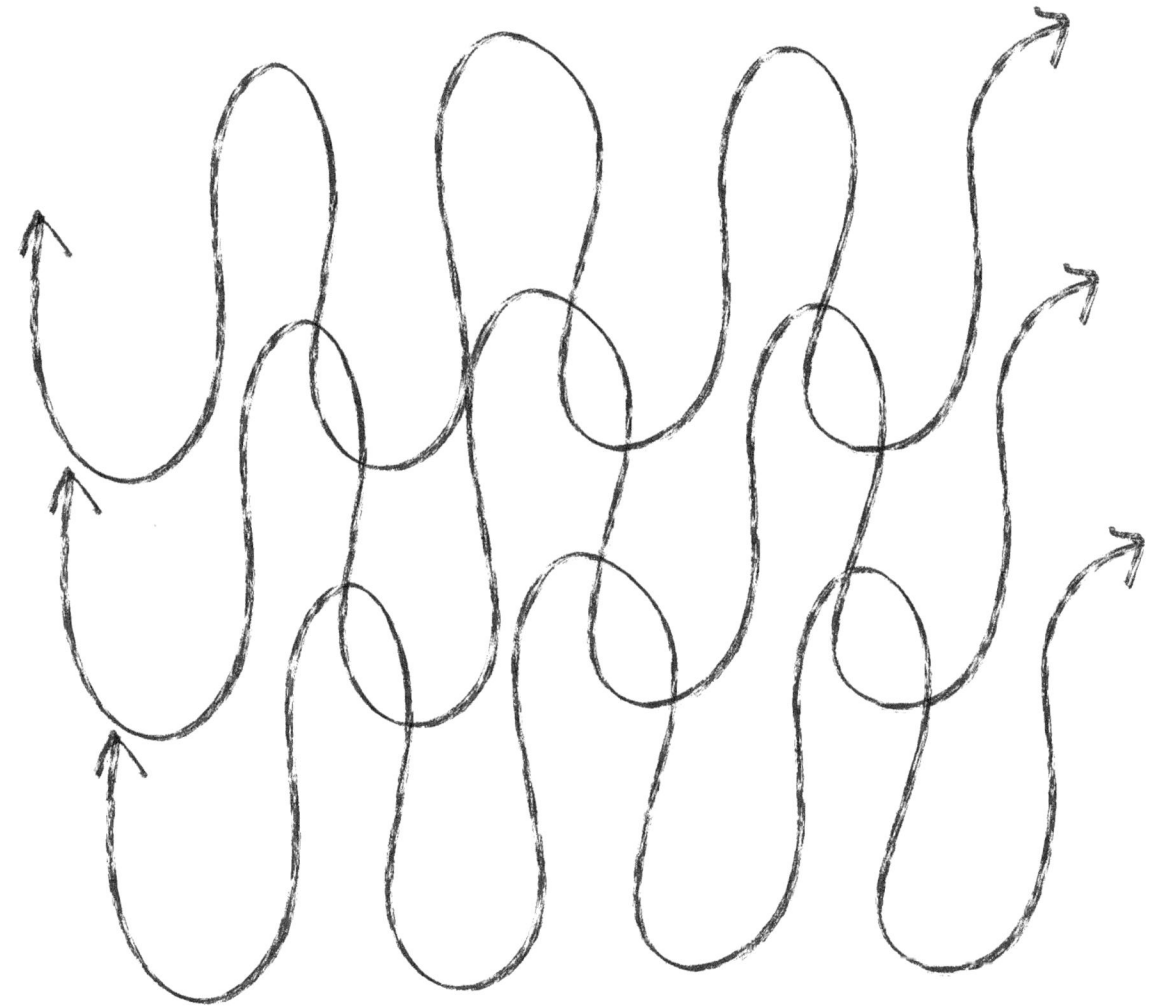

10. Van Riper's asymmetric strategies; not plans.

[#AKA, everyone has a plan, until they are punched in the mouth.]

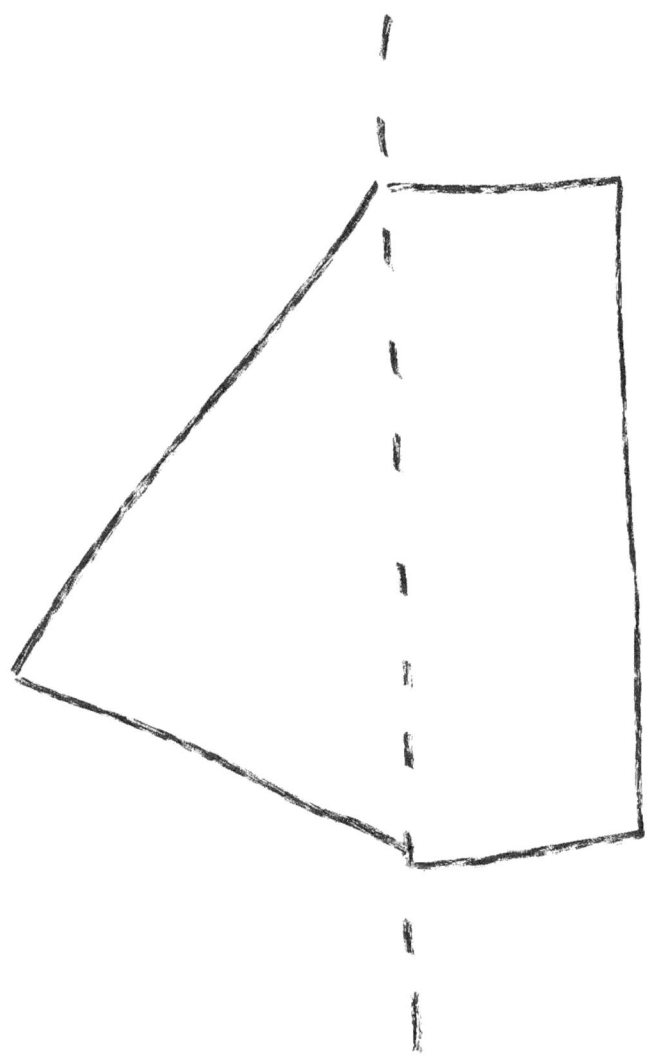

Relationships

1. **Embrace the mantras of humour and helpfulness.**

2. **Understand that your greatest strength is your greatest weakness.**

3. Apply the test of how you would feel if your conduct in a situation went viral on social media.

4. The greatest investment is the ability to communicate.

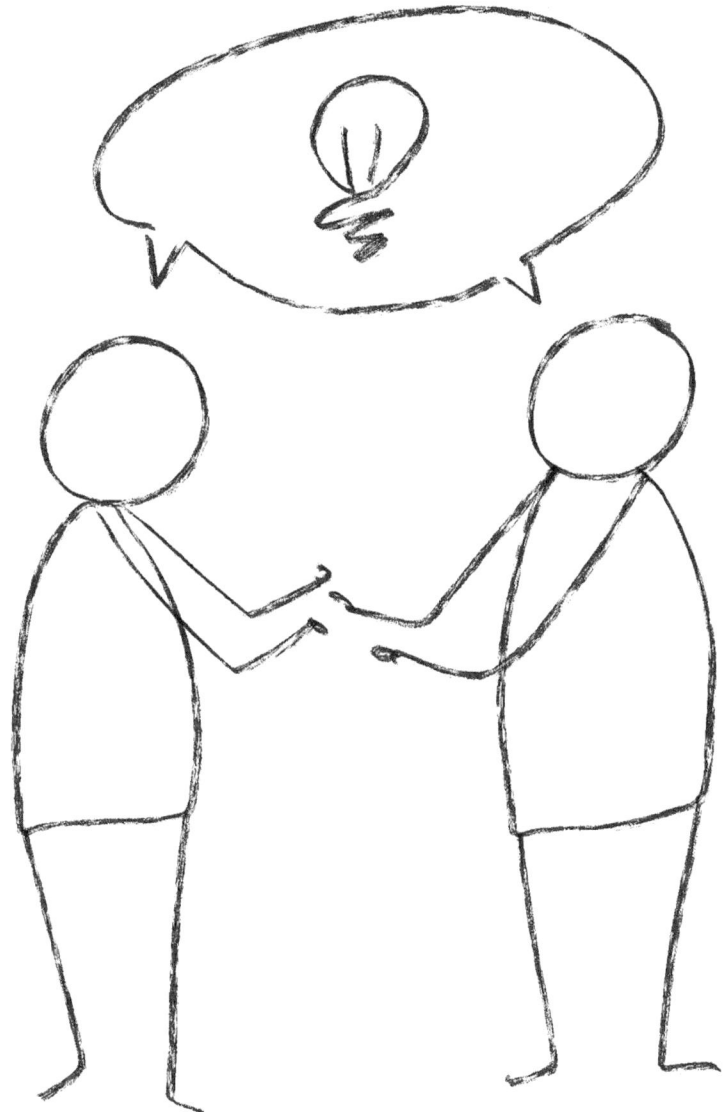

5. Have one full day a week with your loved ones.

6. **Have hobbies around your goals, including family hobbies.**

7. Write gratitude letters and deliver them personally.

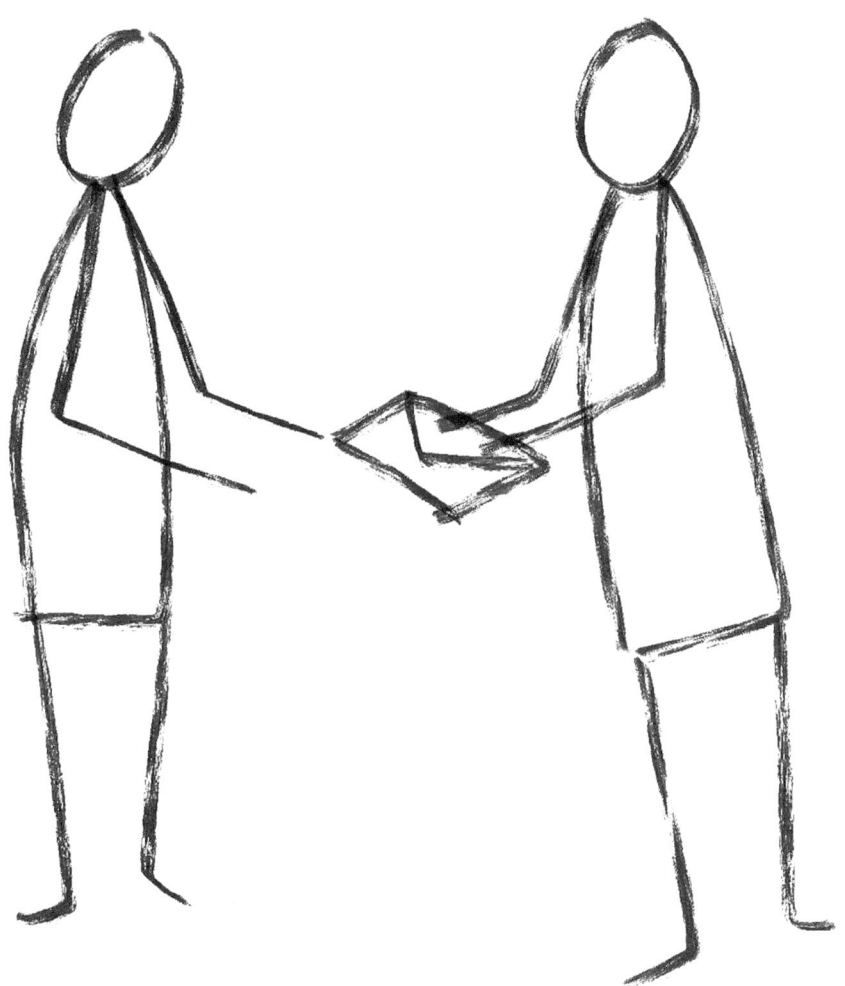

8. Circles of influence.

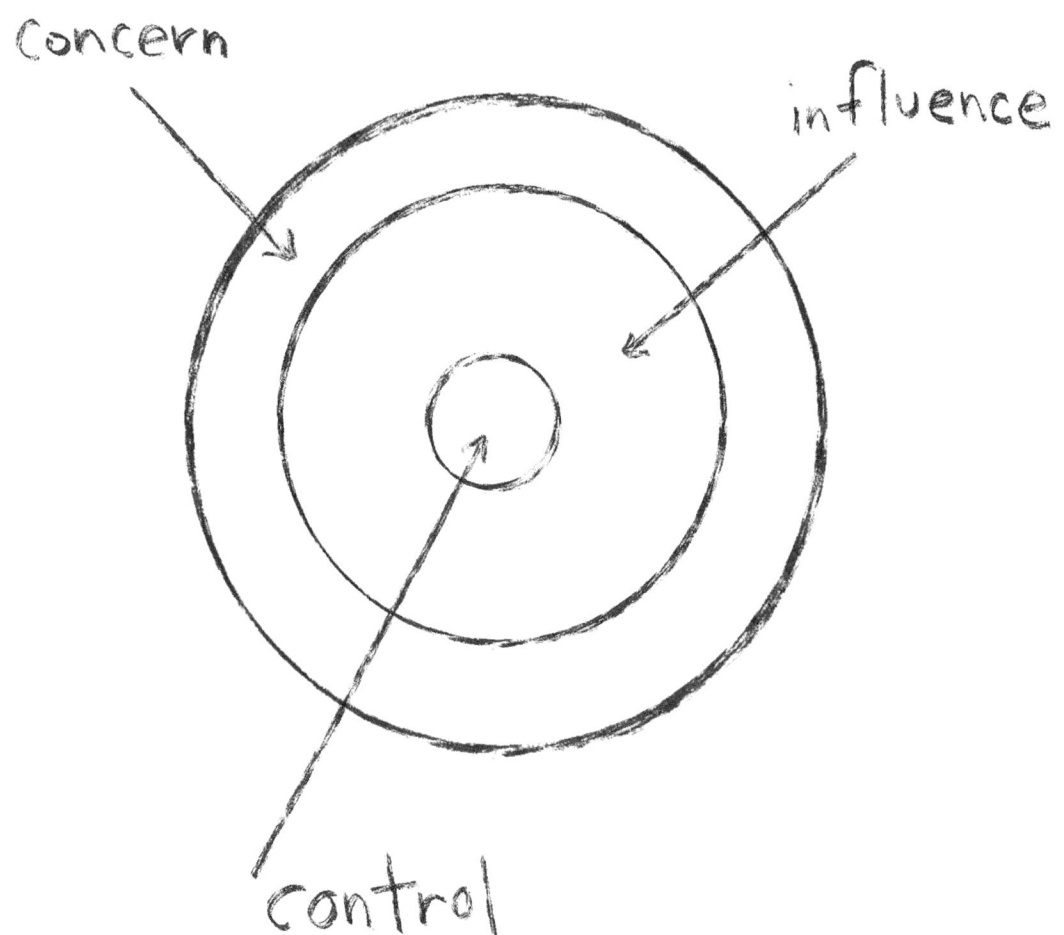

9. 10 minutes early is 10 minutes late.

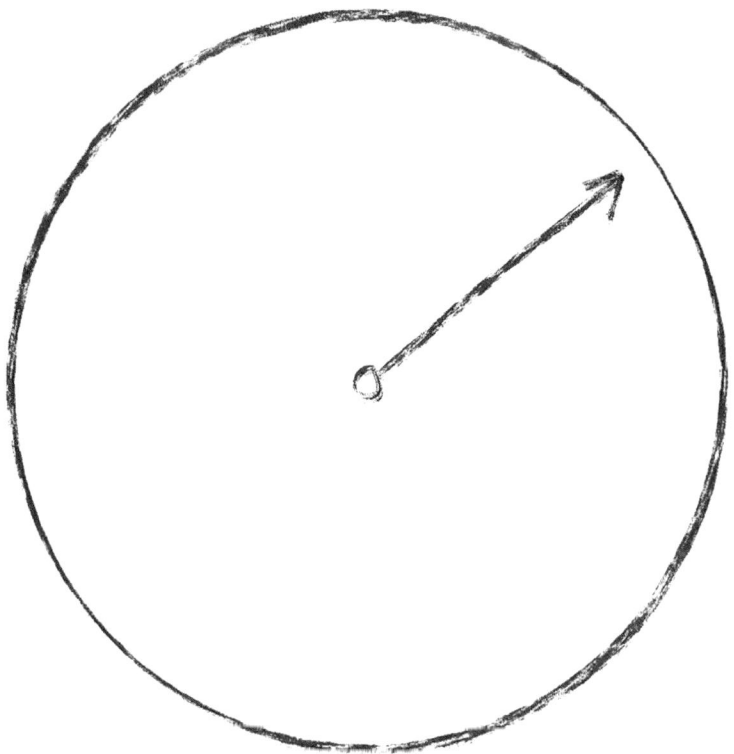

10. Pay for lunch.

Learning

1. **Read at least 50 books a year – ideally batched in one or more short bursts of intense reading.**

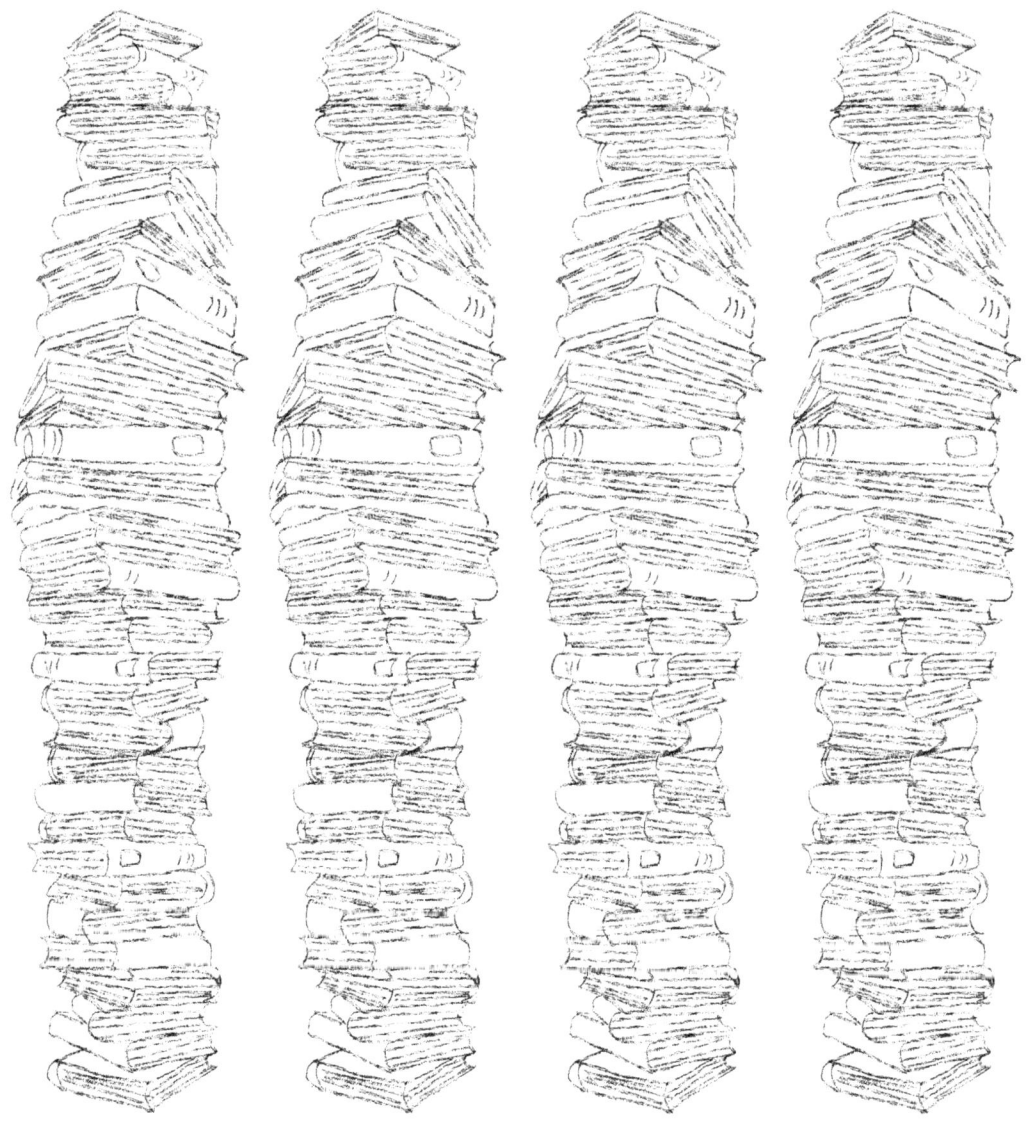

2. Manically take notes – with a pen and paper.

[#If you want to look cool and create opportunities for future serendipity, use a Moleskine and go back through it periodically.]

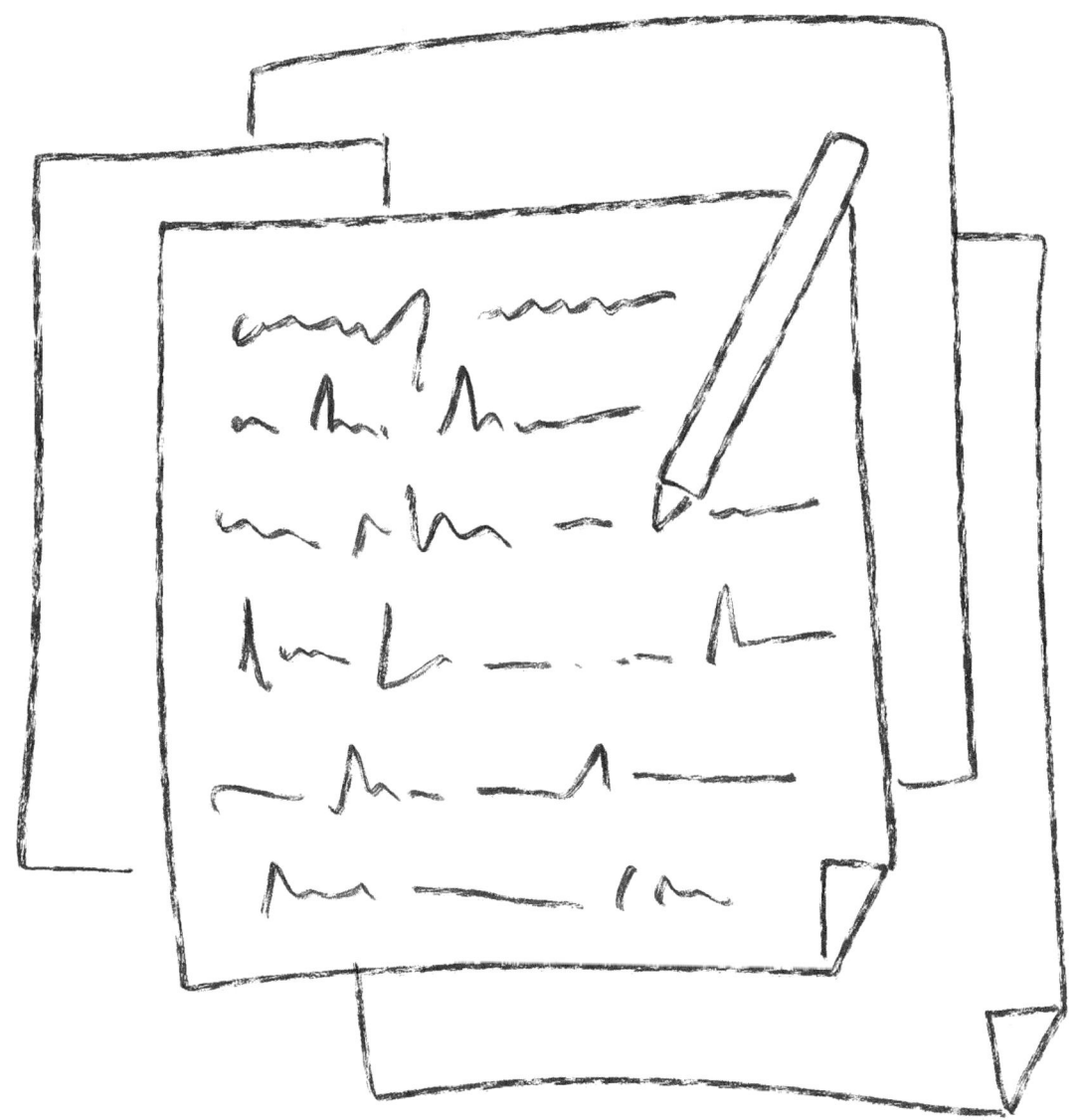

3. **Walk regularly; ensuring you meditate, read or listen to audiobooks, while doing so.**

4. **Tiago Forte's digital system for systematically synthesising past ideas, inspirations, and insights.**

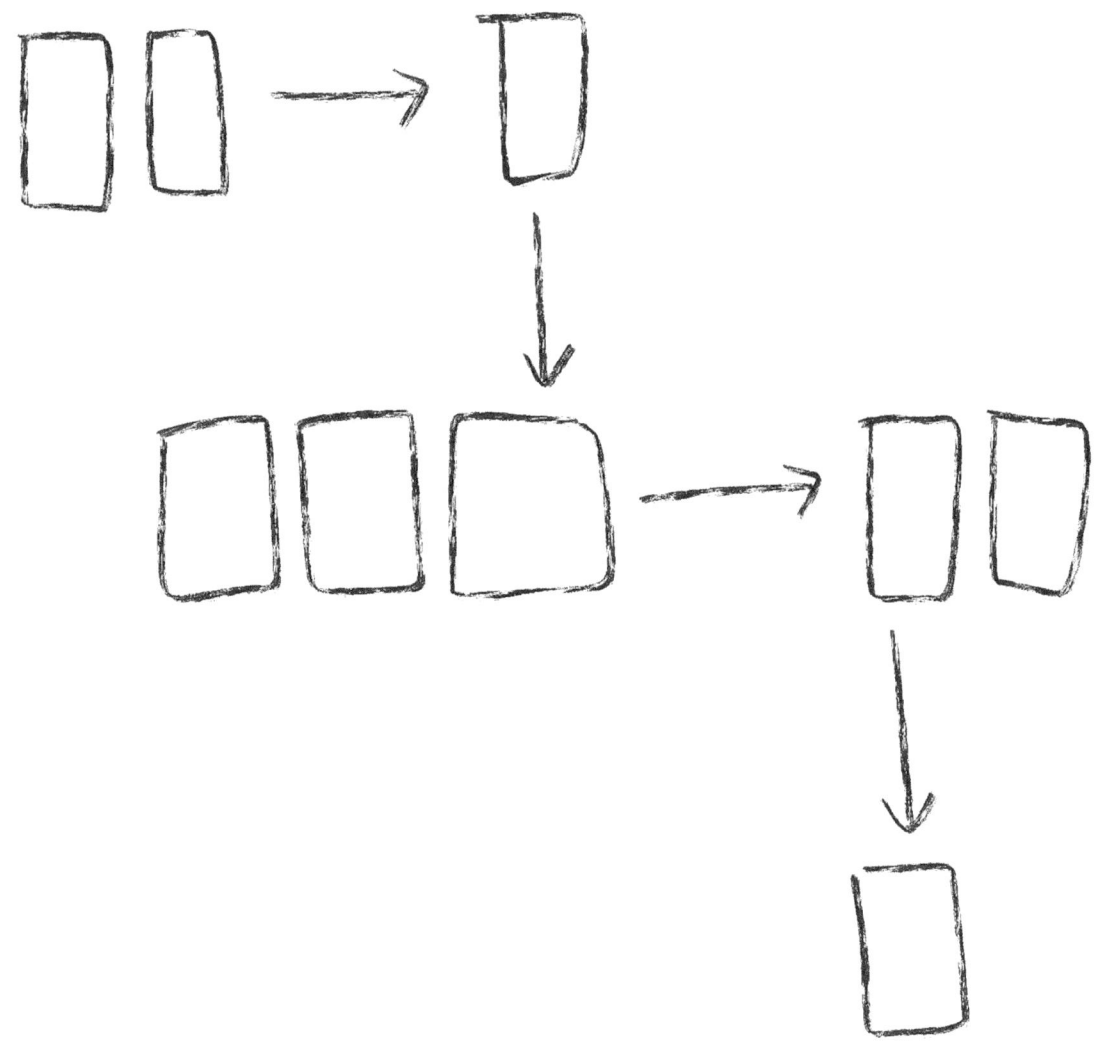

5. Understand the difference in learning modes.

[#Namely visual (spatial), aural (auditory), verbal (linguistic), physical (kinaesthetic), logical (mathematical), social (interpersonal) and solitary (intrapersonal).]

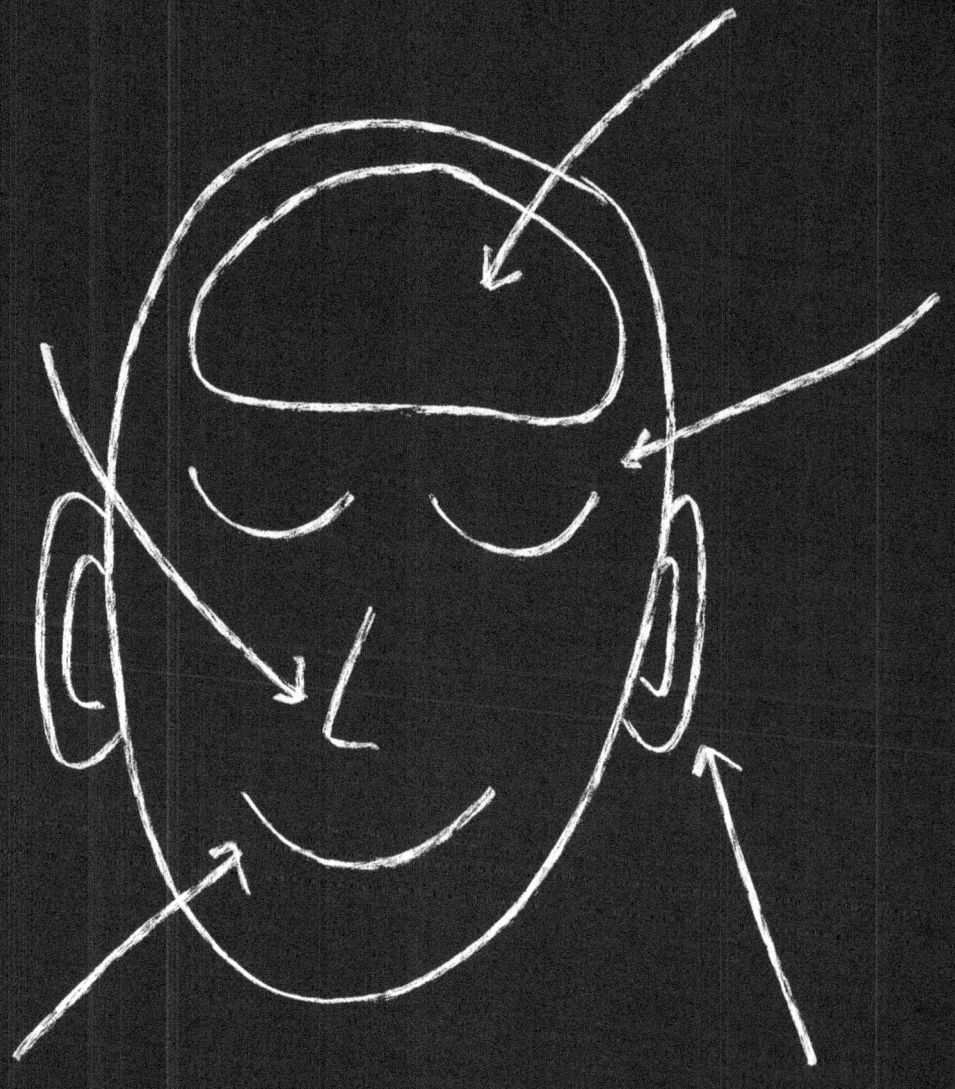

6. **Find what enables you to find flow (e.g. music).**

7. Build your anti-library.

8. Use story, or vision, boards.

9. **Flip it; that is invert, always invert.**

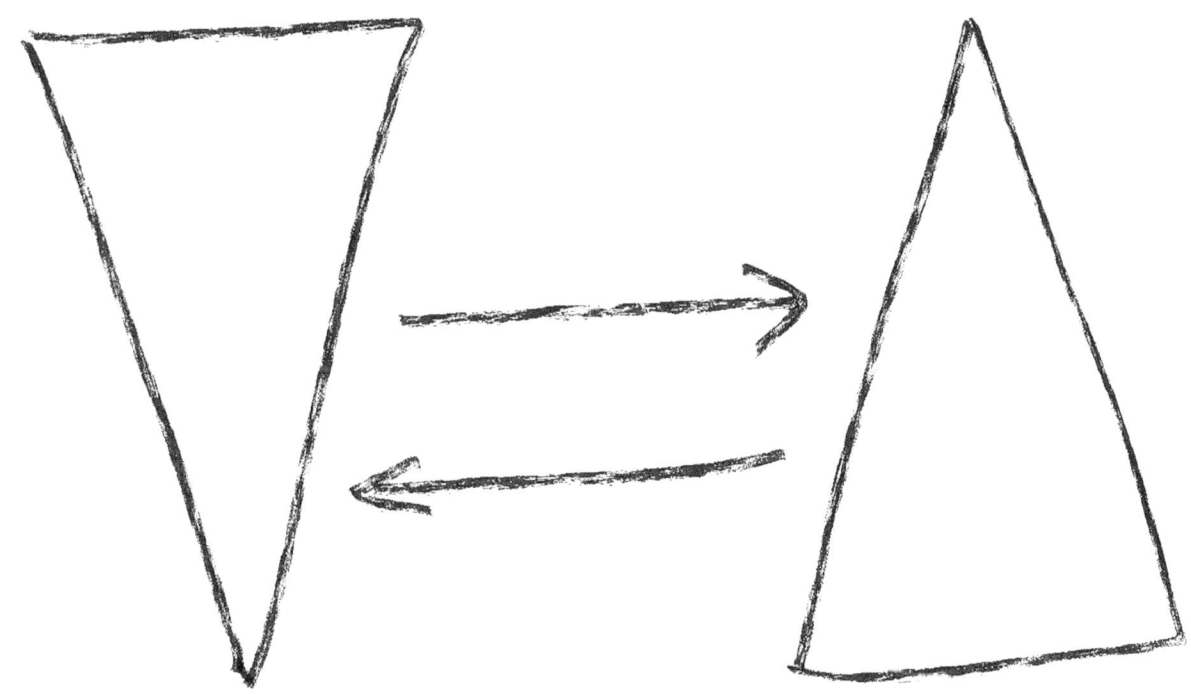

10. Collect your favourite quotes.

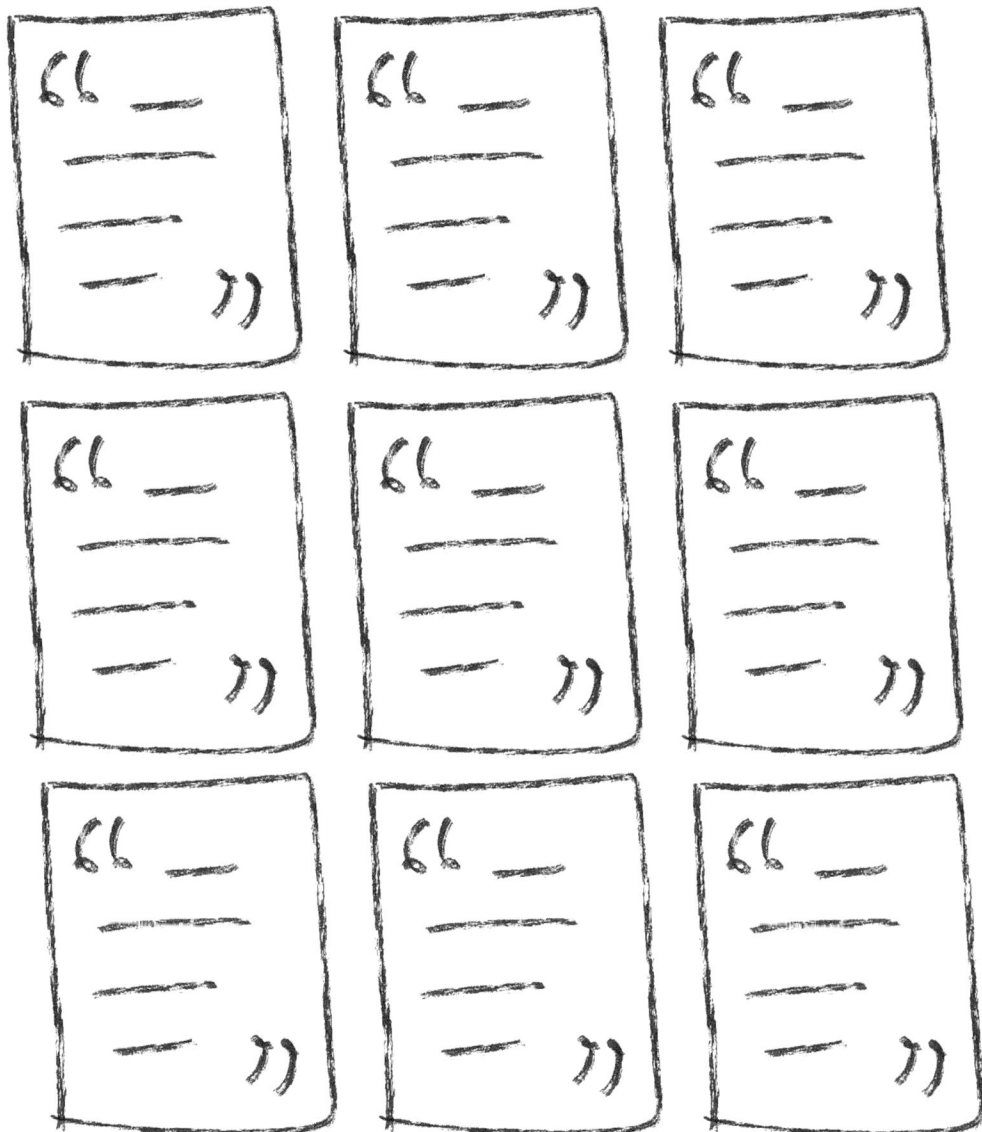

Principles

1. **Barry Schwartz's Paradox of Choice.**

   [#More is less; too much choice creates diminished benefits.]

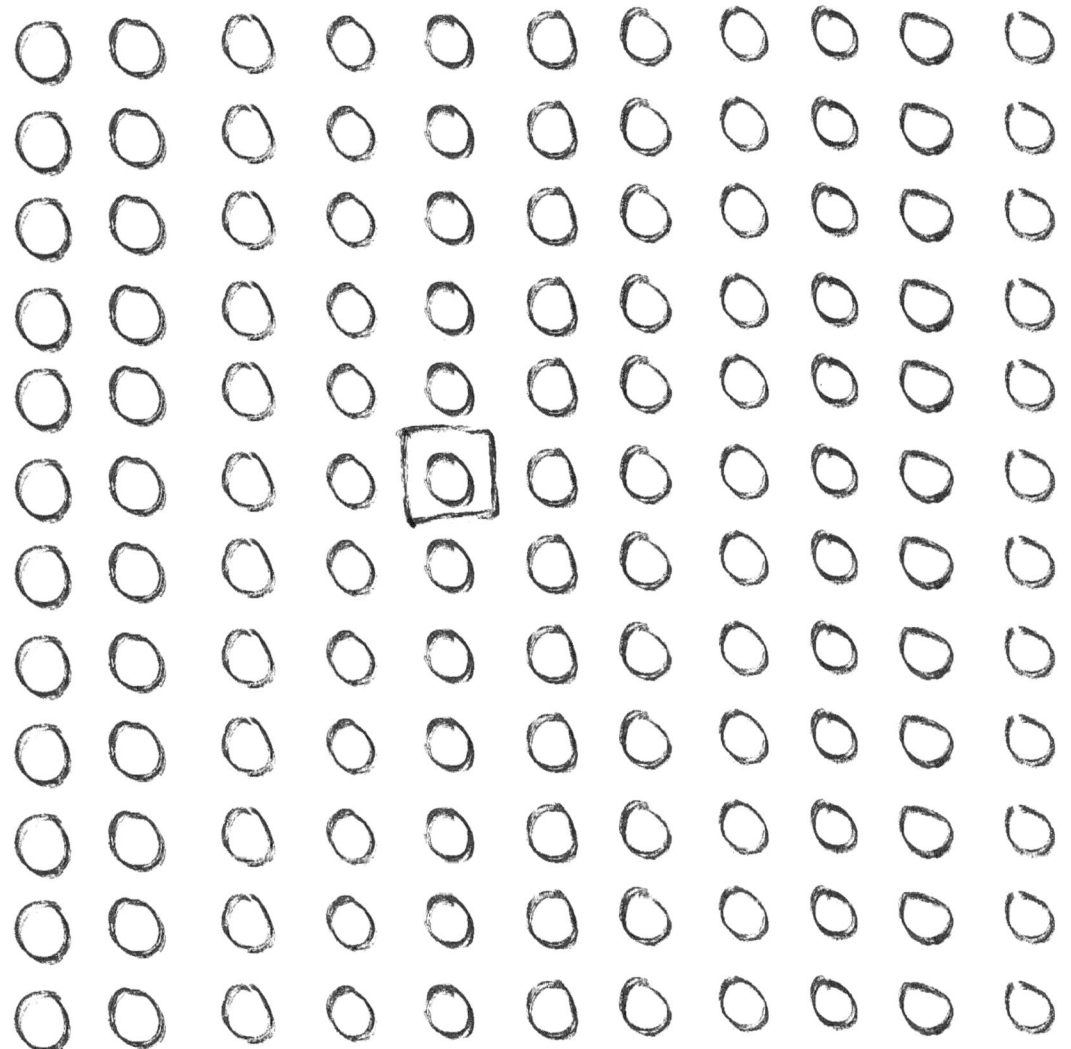

2. Parkinson's Law

[#Tasks expand to fill available time.]

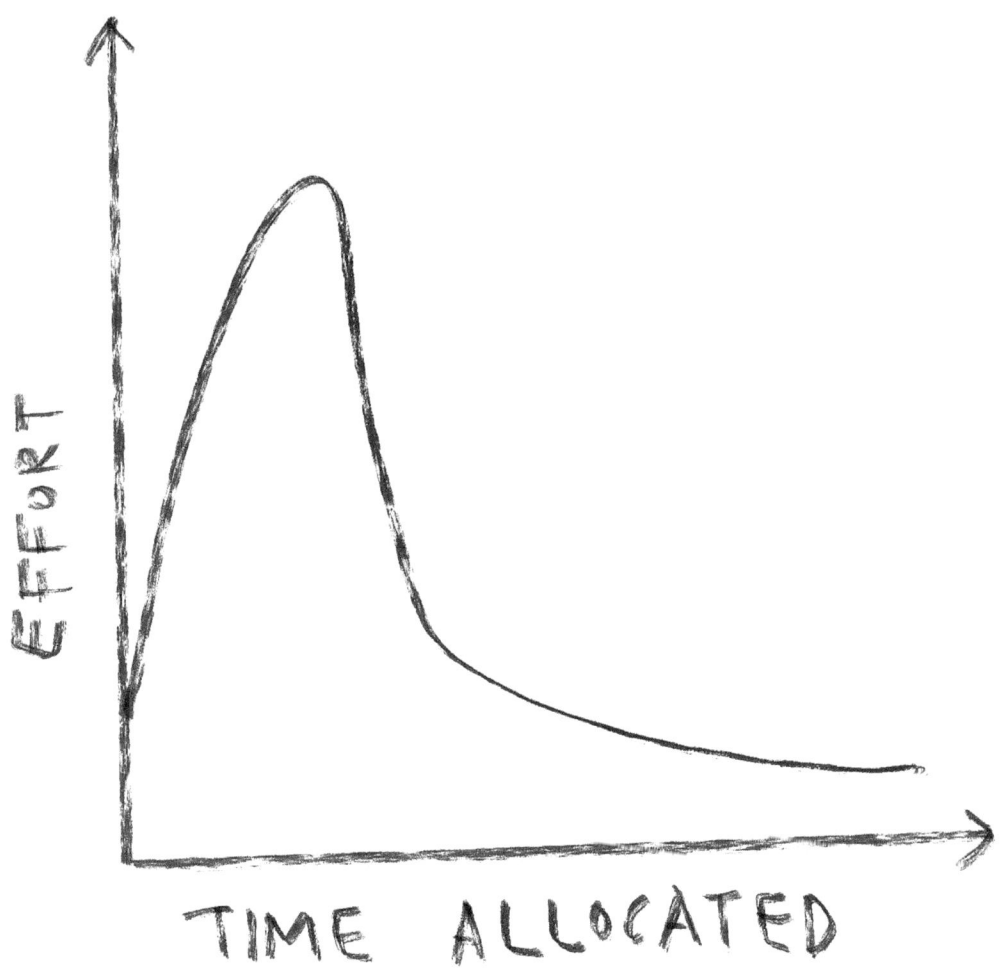

Pareto Principle

[#80% of outcomes are due to 20% of the inputs.]

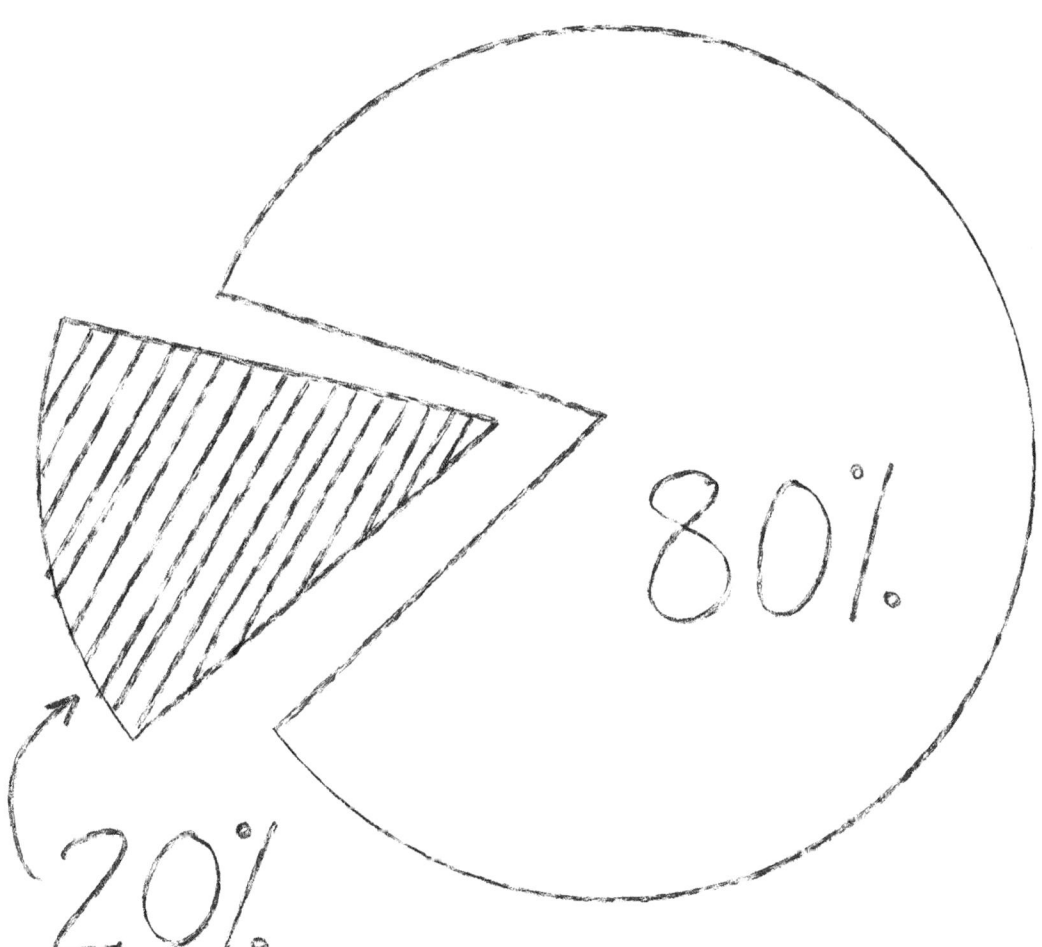

Peter Principle

[#When someone is promoted to their level of incompetence.]

Paul Principle

[#When someone is promoted out of the position in which they can do the most damage.]

6. Bloch's Axiom

[#You will spend longer looking for something than the time it would have taken to simply recreate it.]

Cohn's Law

[#Bureaucracy is about paperwork increasing evermore; with ever less actual work. Stability arrives when 100% of resources are spent reporting on absolutely nothing.]

8. Anderson's Axiom

[#You can only be young once; but you can be immature forever.]

9. Nassim Taleb's: Skin in the Game

[#Having a measurable risk when making a major decision is necessary for fairness.]

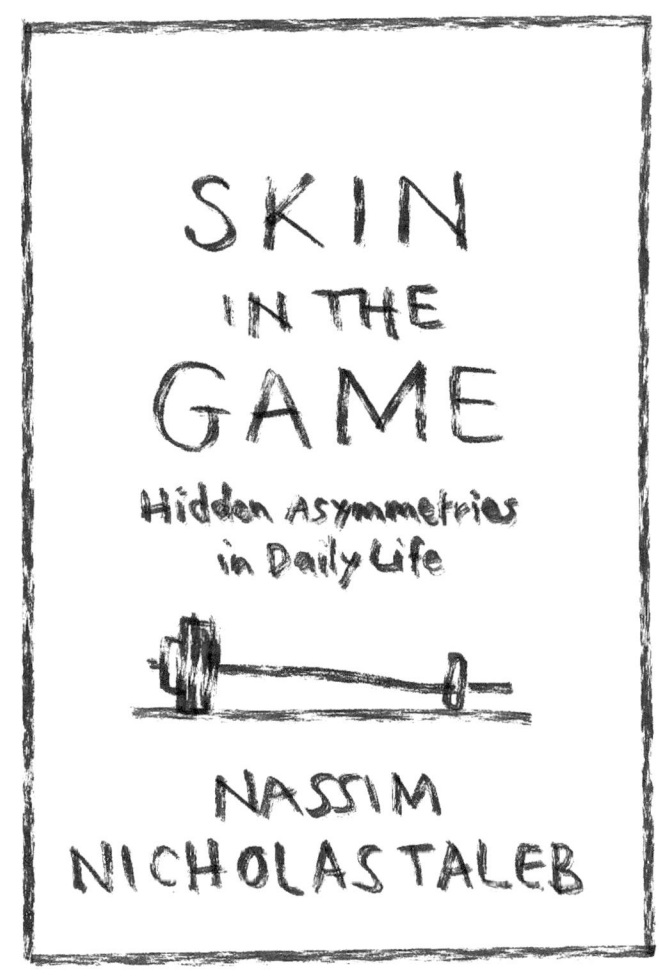

10. Believe in the Butterfly Effect

[#A small change in one state of deterministic nonlinear systems can result in large differences at a later stage.]

Tech

1. Religiously use folders in your email inbox and have the discipline to check them every month.

Listen to audiobooks (including podcasts) on at least double speed, even up to 3 or 3.5 speed.

[#Tricky when you meet these people in real life.]

3. Dictate everything.

[#If you feel as though it is too short, batch the work, and ensure that the transcription team has direct access to your draft box.]

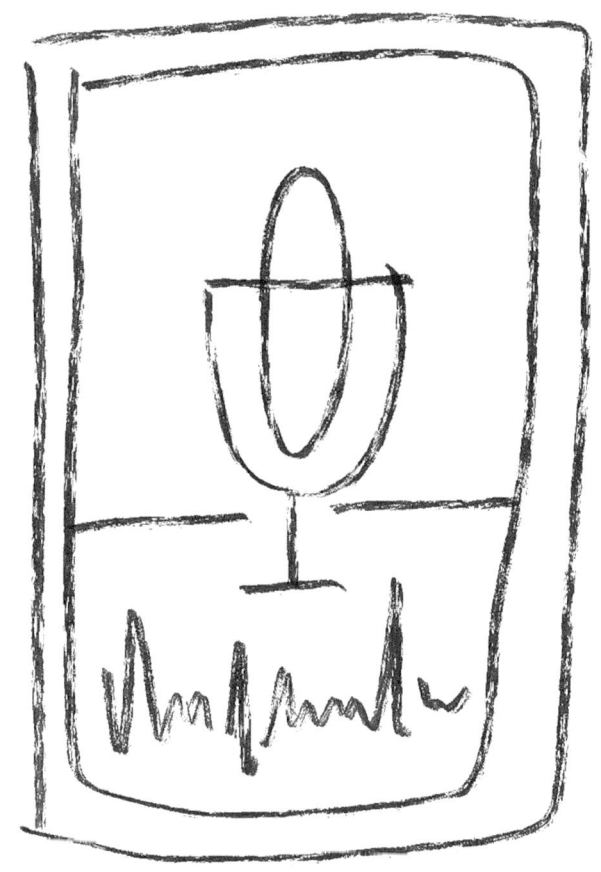

4. **Turn off all notifications, including sound, on all devices, and turn on greyscale for your smart devices.**

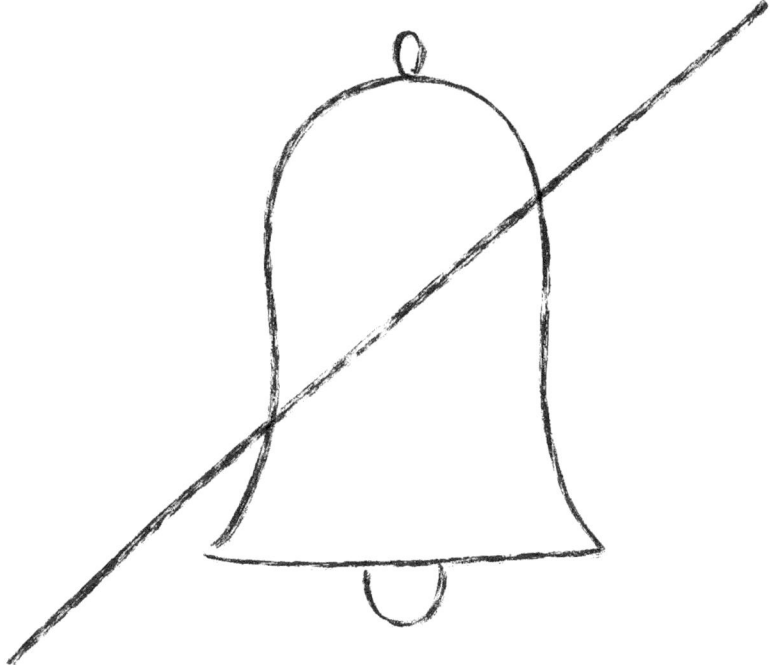

5. **Actively look to habit iterate; for example, replace social media hits by reading a chapter of a book.**

6. Peter Diamandis' 6Ds:

a. Digitisation
b. Disruption
c. Dematerialise (from physical to digital)
d. Demonetisation – i.e. the dropping of price
e. Democratisation – access for all
f. Deceptive – at first there seems to be no growth

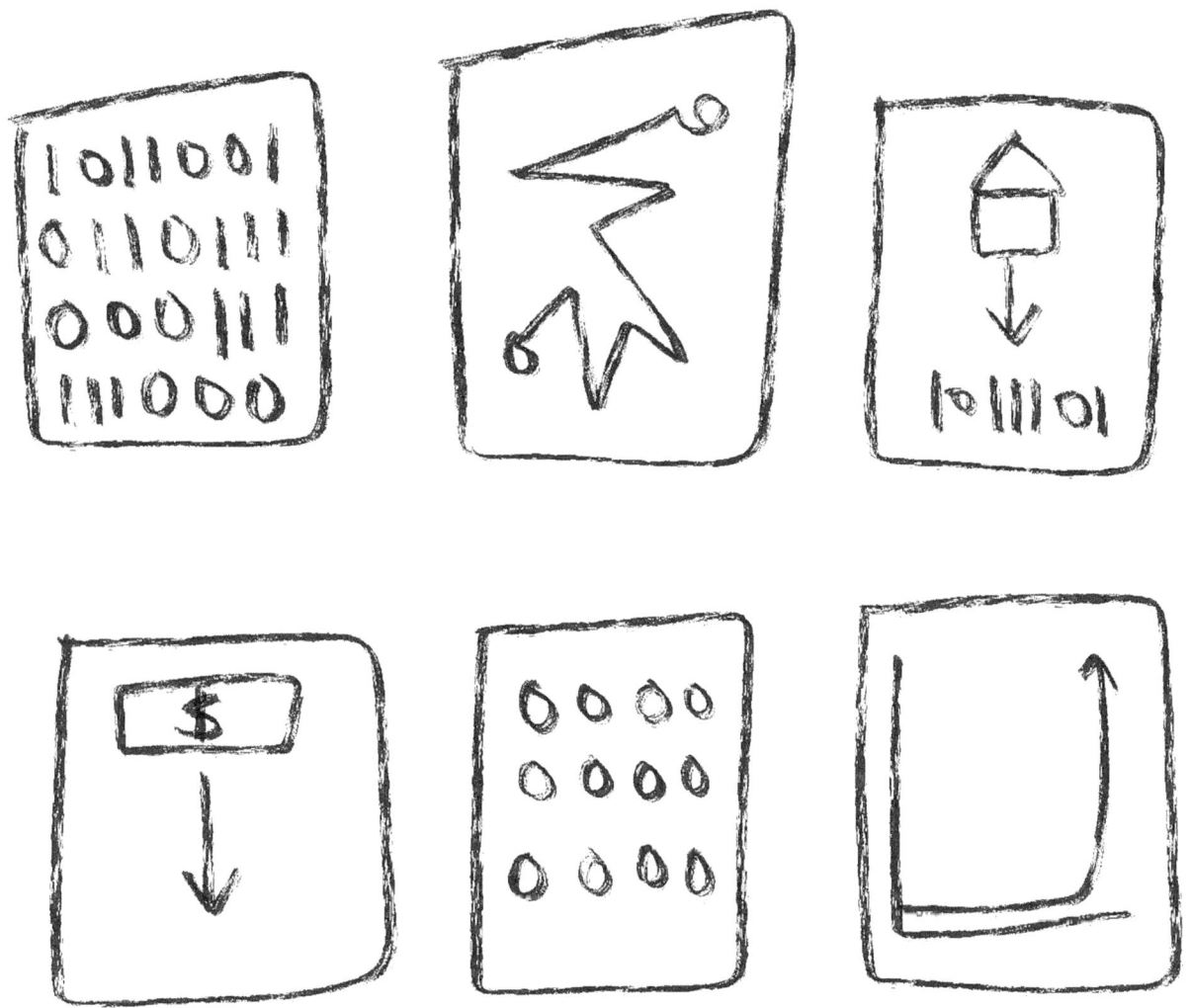

7. **Fast, frictionless, fun and free.**

8. Print it.

Upwork. Fiverr. Airtasker.

[#AKA delegate with discipline.]

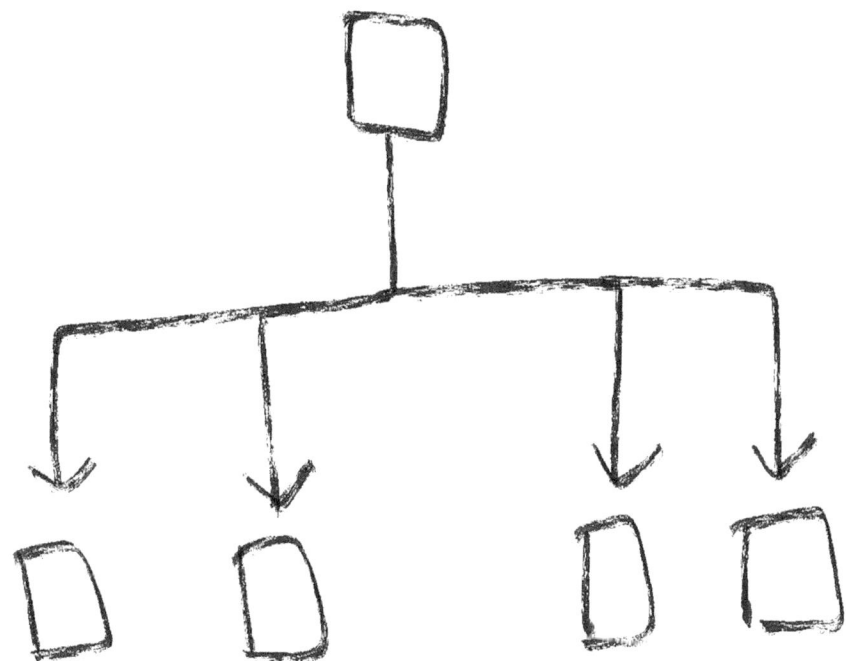

10. Make everything as simple as possible; however no simpler.

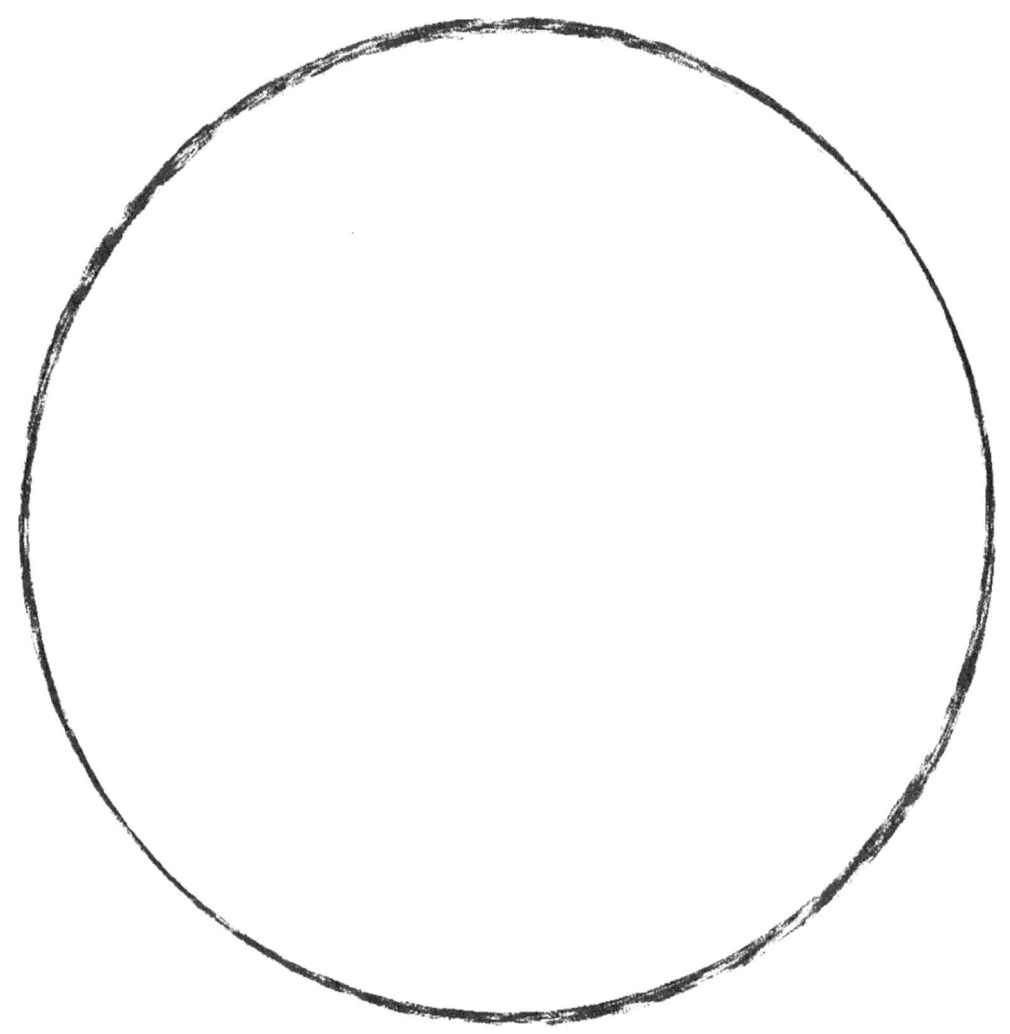

Frameworks

1. **Why is it not WD 39?**

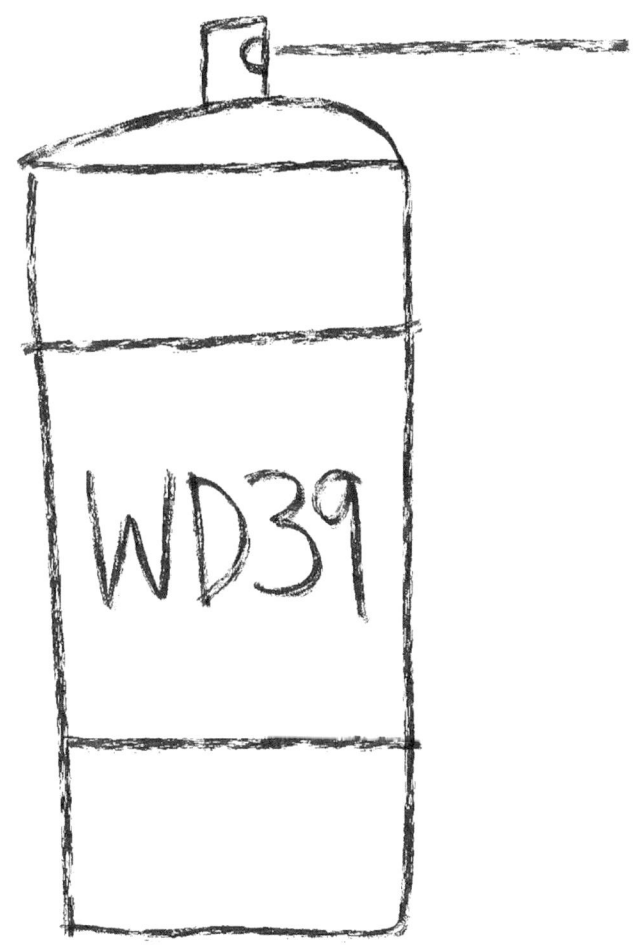

2. **The meaning of life is meaning.**

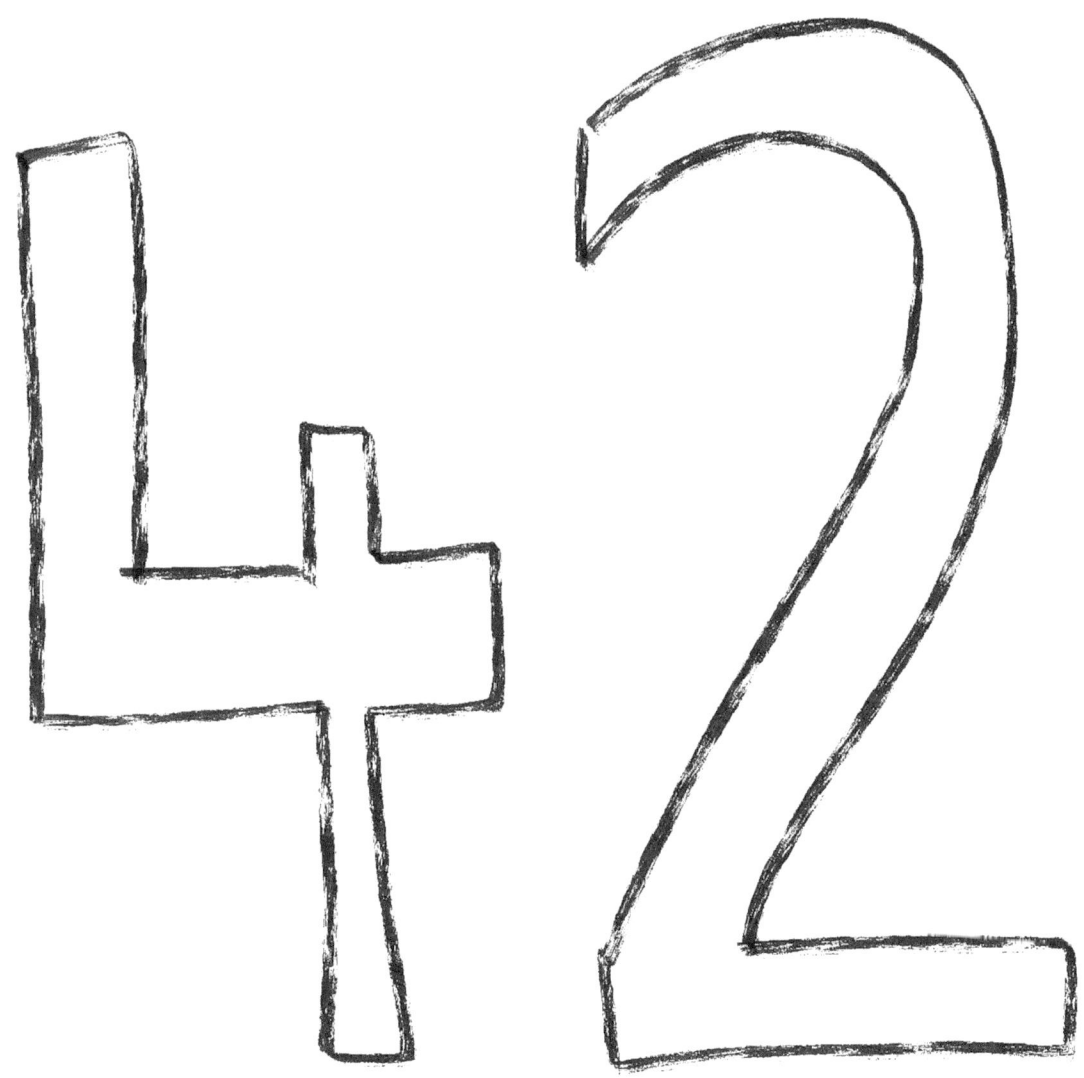

3. **Common sense; is uncommon.**

4. **Silence is golden.**

[#You have two ears and one mouth. Use them in those proportions.]

5. Write your Life Handbook (this is ours).

6. **Have a BHAV (Big Hairy Audacious Vision).**

7. Planning is more important than the activity.

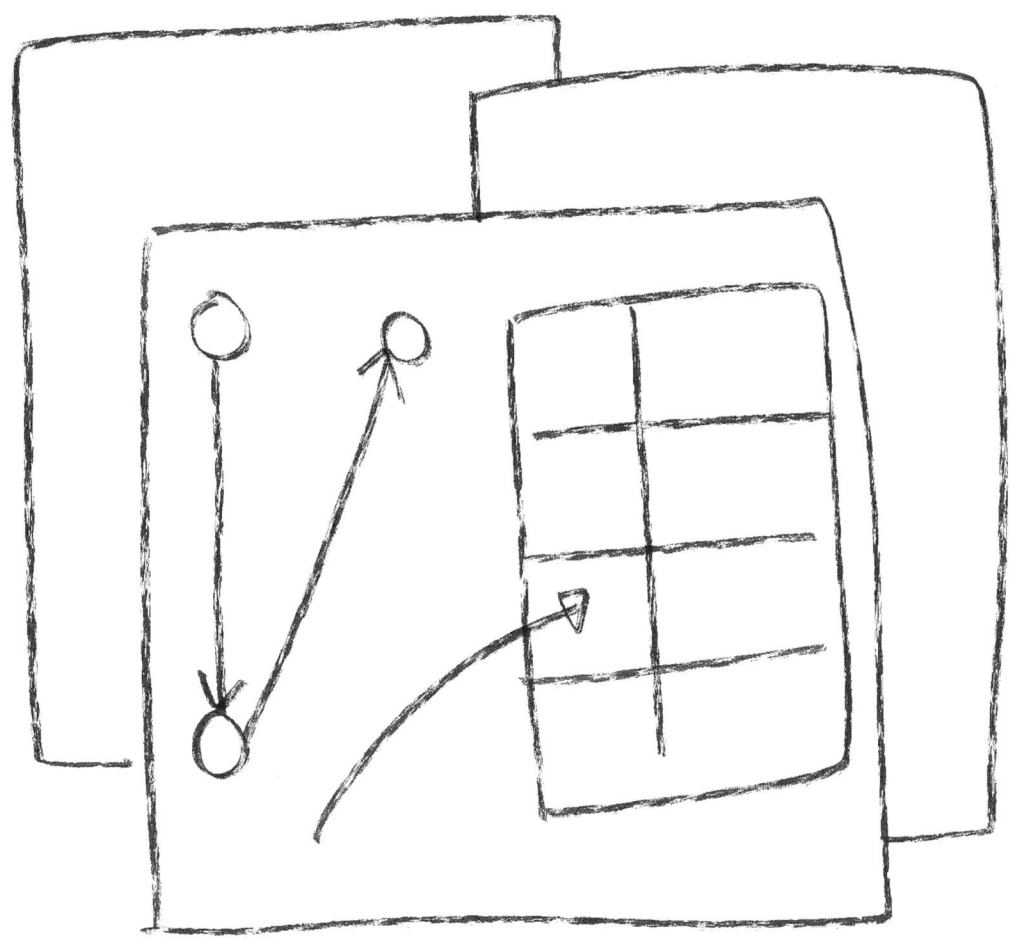

8. Walk into the room of mirrors.

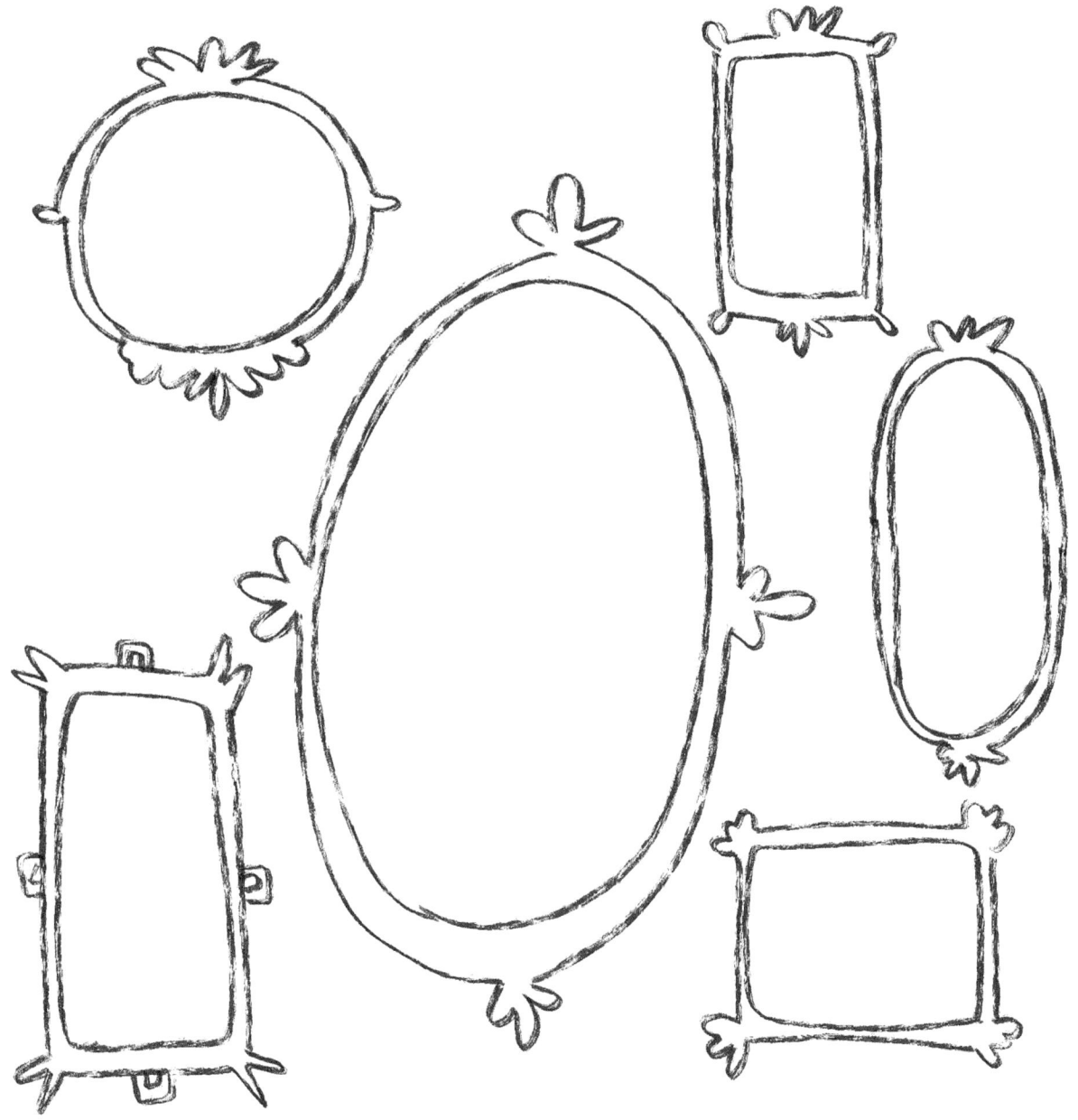

9. **Get back up one more time than the next person – move from failure to failure without the loss of enthusiasm.**

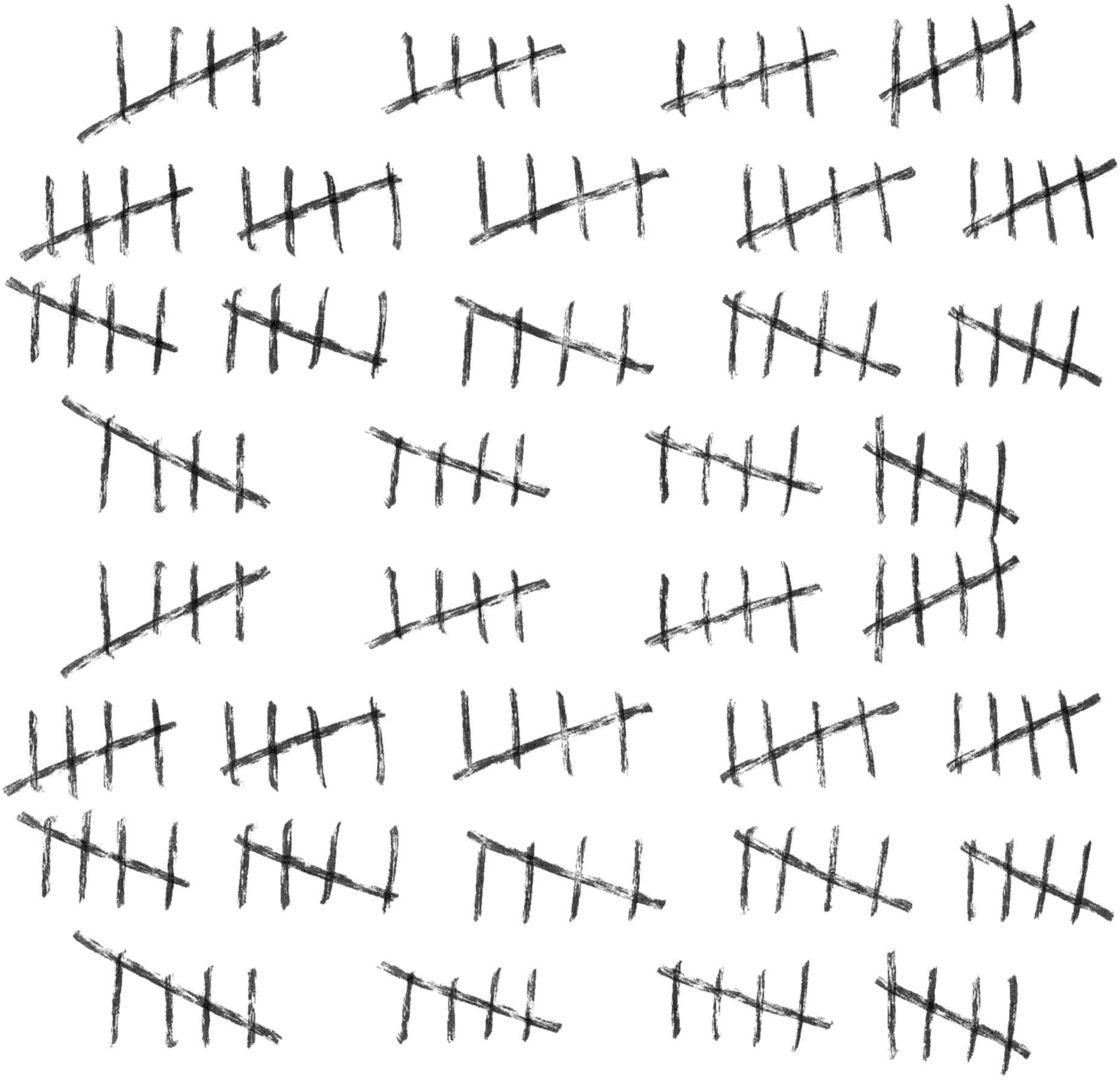

10. It is the journey, not the destination.

Tips

1. **Understand that it normally takes at least 10 years to become an overnight success.**

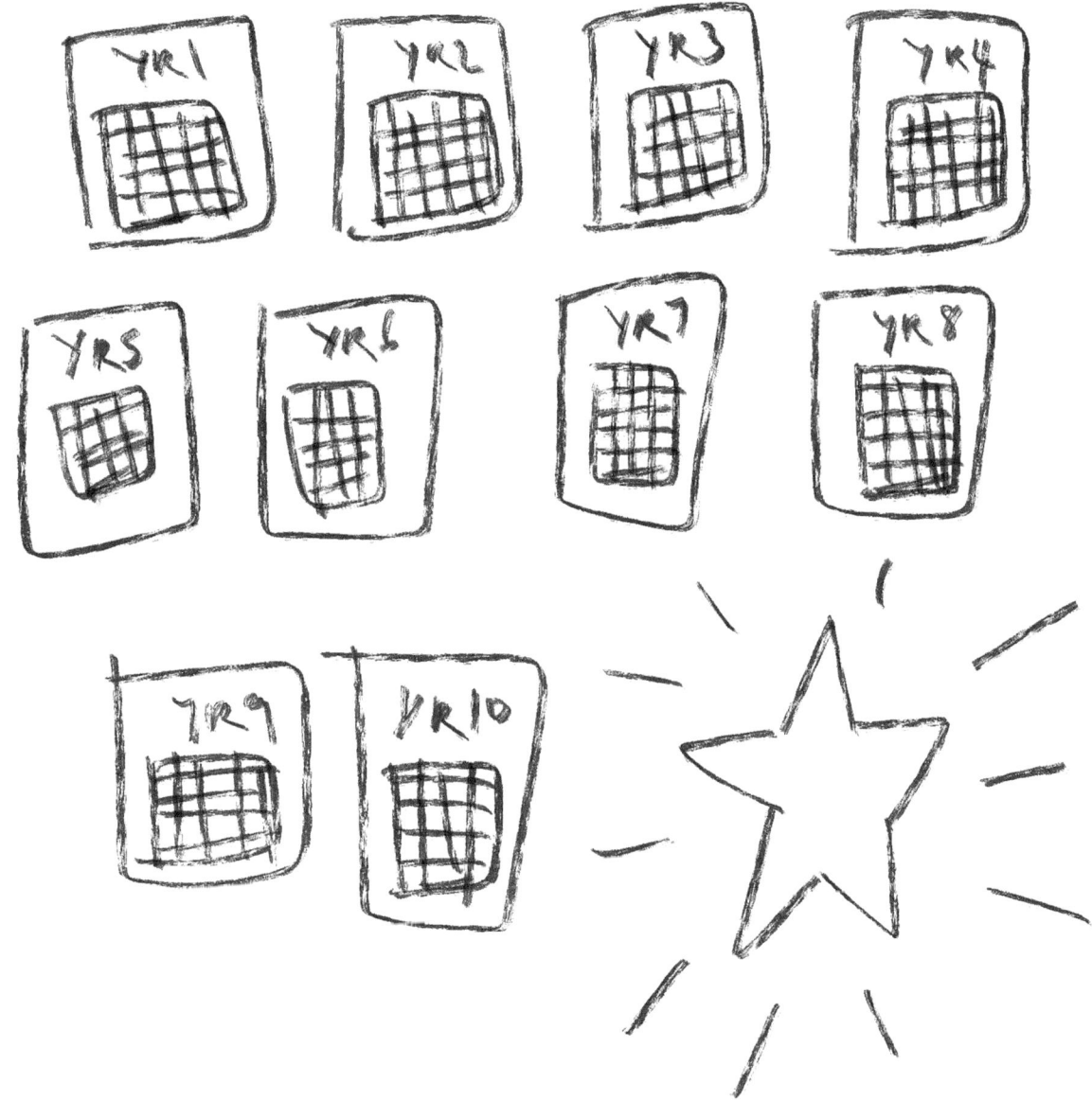

2. Excellence comes from being uncomfortable.

If you want what the 1% have, you need to do what 99% won't.

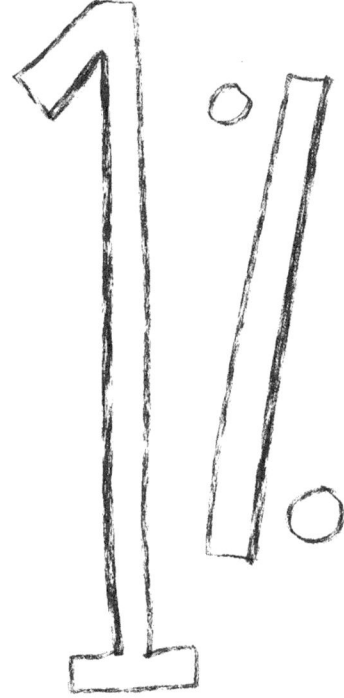

4. Charlie Munger's 25 Tendencies of Human Misjudgement.

Poor Charlie's Almanack

The Wit and Wisdom of
CHARLES T. MUNGER

5. **Live like you will die tomorrow. Learn like you will live forever.**

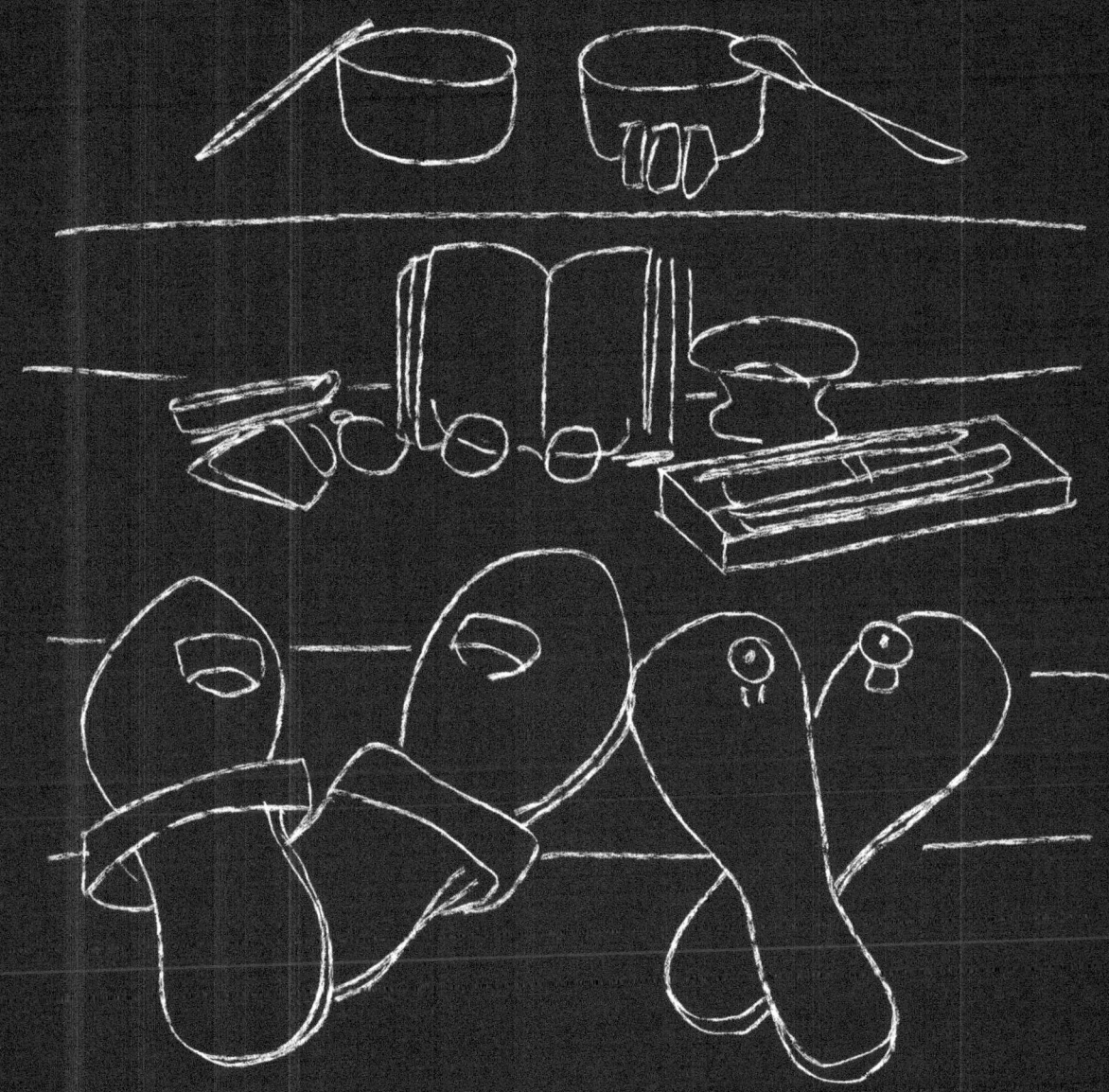

6. **To begin with success, start at the end.**

7. Be prepared.

8. Aim for the stars.

9. **Reverse psychology is a thing.**

10. Less. Is. More.

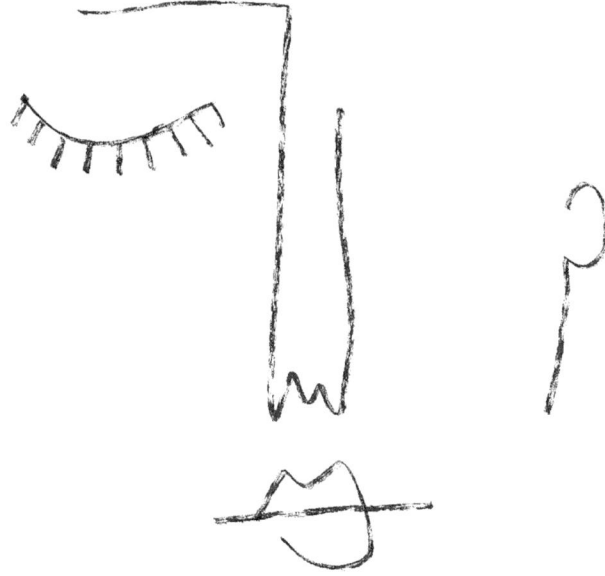

and some more...

Idea Initiators

CHAPTER 1 – HEALTH

1. No technology within the last 60 minutes of each day. See: *Expert Guide to Sleeping Well* by Chris Idzikowski
2. Do not use an alarm to wake up unless you absolutely have to. See: *Predictably Irrational* by Dan Ariely
3. Travel the night before; be where you need to be and ready. See: *Eat That Frog!: 21 Great Ways to Stop Procrastinating and Get More Done in Less Time* by Brian Tracy
4. Sleep. 8. Hours. See: *Eat Move Sleep: How Small Choices Lead to Big Changes* by Tom Rath
5. Green smoothies. See: *Green for Life* by Victoria Boutenko
6. Great shoes and a great bed. See: *Why We Sleep* by Matthew Walker
7. Walking adventures. Hat tip: the 'Gemba Walk' developed by Toyota (also known as 'management by walking around').
8. Breathe. Through. Your. Nose. See: *The Oxygen Advantage* by Patrick McKeown
9. Early to bed, early to rise, work hard and exercise. Hat tip: Ted Turner quote 'Early to bed, early to rise, work like hell, and advertise'
10. Find ways to have regular breaks and ideally leverage them into where you otherwise want to be. See: *Alchemy* by Rory Sutherland

CHAPTER 2 – MENTORING

1. Develop and foster at least one mastermind group in real life and another mastermind group in your dreams. See: *Think and Grow Rich* by Napoleon Hill
2. Share a meal with your family and loved ones at least once a day, around a table; sans devices. See: *Seven Habits of Highly Effective People* by Stephen Covey
3. Proactively have guests to your family dinner. Hat tip: leading corporate lawyer Brett Heading

4. Actively look for coaches and mentors in books and in your tribe. See: *Coach: Lessons on the Game of Life* by Michael Lewis
5. Pay it forward. See: *Pay it Forward* by Catherine Ryan Hyde
6. Have heroes. See: *The Hero with a Thousand Faces* by Joseph Campbell
7. Reverse mentoring – the younger they are the less information they have to remove before learning. See: *Why Reverse Mentoring Works and How to Do It Right (Harvard Business Review)* by Jennifer Jordan and Michael Sorell
8. The only measure you need for your life: the impact you have on others. See: *How will you measure your life* by Clayton Christensen
9. Fitzgerald's Intelligence Test: the ability to hold two opposed ideas in mind at the same time and still retain the ability to function. See: "The Crack Up", Esquire Magazine (February 1936) by F. Scott Fitzgerald (author of books such as *The Great Gatsby*)
10. Quality time is accessed only via quantity time. See: *3 Reasons Why "Quality Time over Quantity Time" Is Not True for Parents (and Leaders)* by Eric Geiger

CHAPTER 3 – HABITS

1. Meditation and focused thinking. See: *Headspace* by Andy Puddicombe
2. Embrace start times at, for example, 10 minutes past the hour. Hat tip: b1g1 founder Paul Dunn
3. Multi leverage – for example swimming and meditation. See: *The Four Hour Body* by Tim Ferriss
4. Understand multitasking is only possible with one focused activity, however, look for ways to leverage this – for example doing conference calls while walking. See: *Steve Jobs* by Walter Isaacson
5. Find exercise routines that are unbreakable – for example, do not rely on third parties or external equipment – planking is a great example. See: *Overcoming Gravity: A Systematic Approach to Gymnastics and Bodyweight Strength* by Steven Low
6. Do the easy things; and your life will be hard. See: *Secrets of the Millionaire Mind - Mastering the Inner Game of Wealth* by T. Harv Eker
7. Embrace storytelling. See: *Winning the Story Wars* by Jonah Sachs
8. Bucket list. See: *The Bucket List* by Justin Zackham
9. Live like a Stoic for a week. See: *Learn Modern Stoicism* by Donald Robertson
10. Have perfect posture and vocal strength. Hat tip: TPI founder Torb Pedersen

CHAPTER 4 – THINKING

1. Batch all work. Small tasks can be bundled up. Large tasks should be chunked down. See: *Work Smarter Not Harder* by Jack Collis and Michael LeBoeuf
2. Understand the distinction between holidays and travel. Hat tip: Matthew's mum
3. Understand the power of and (not or) – in particular loose and tight. See: *In Search of Excellence* by Tom Peters and Robert H. Waterman, Jr
4. Questions; not answers are the key. Michael Bungay Stanier's 7 coaching questions:
   a. Kickstart Question - What's on your mind?
   b. AWE Question - And What Else?
   c. Focus Question - What's the real challenge here for you?
   d. Foundation Question - What do you want?
   e. Lazy Question - How can I help?
   f. Strategic Question - If you're saying yes to this, what are you saying no to?
   g. Learning Question - What was most useful to you about this conversation?
5. Nathaniel Branden's six pillars of self-esteem:
   a. Be conscious, listen deeply, be present (an un-anxious presence)
   b. Self-acceptance – including accepting feelings and thinking about them
   c. Self-responsibility – autonomy, freedom and accountability – they are all the same thing
   d. Self-assertiveness – respecting your rights and the rights of others and be halfway between passive and aggressive
   e. Living purposefully – starting with why
   f. Personal integrity – your character is your destiny
6. Maria Popova's 10 learnings:
   a. Allow yourself the uncomfortable luxury of changing your mind
   b. Do nothing for prestige or status or money or approval alone (or 'Would you rather be the world's greatest lover, but have everyone think you're the world's worst lover? Or would you rather be the world's worst lover but have everyone think you're the world's greatest lover?')
   c. Be generous
   d. Build pockets of stillness into your life

    e. When people tell you who they are, believe them. When people try to tell you who you are, don't believe them
    f. Presence is far more intricate and rewarding an art than productivity
    g. Expect anything worthwhile to take a long time
    h. Seek out what magnifies your spirit
    i. Embrace being an idealist
    j. Fight cynicism

7. Embrace the eighth wonder of the world – compounding. See: *The Snowball: Warren Buffett and the Business of Life* by Alice Schroeder
8. Allow serendipity to occur. See: *How to Not Find What You're Looking For (in The Scientific American)* by Karla Starr
9. Foster synchronicity. See: *Synchronicity* by Carl Jung
10. Van Riper's asymmetric strategies; not plans (AKA, everyone has a plan, until they are punched in the mouth). See: *The lost lesson of Millennium Challenge 2002, the Pentagon's embarrassing post-9/11 war game* by Francis Horton and Hat tip: Mike Tyson

CHAPTER 5 – RELATIONSHIPS

1. Embrace the mantras of humour and helpfulness. See: *Seriously Playful and Playfully Serious: The Helpfulness of Humorous Parody* by Michael Richard Lucas
2. Understand that your greatest strength is your greatest weakness. Hat tip: William Shakespeare
3. Apply the test of how you would feel if your conduct in a situation went viral on social media. Hat tip: Every introductory ethics course at law school
4. The greatest investment is the ability to communicate. See: *How to Win Friends and Influence People* by Dale Carnegie
5. Have one full day a week with your loved ones. Hat tip: Capital Airport Group founder Terry Snow
6. Have hobbies around your goals, including family hobbies. See: *Overwhelmed: Work, Love, and Play When No One Has the Time* by Brigid Schulte
7. Write gratitude letters and deliver them personally. See: *A Whole New Mind* by Daniel Pink

8. Circles of influence. See: The Serenity Prayer by Reinhold NiebuhrIt, namely: "Grant me the serenity to accept the things I cannot change, courage to change the things I can, and wisdom to know the difference"
9. 10 minutes early is 10 minutes late. Hat tip: author and speaker Keith Abraham
10. Pay for lunch. Hat tip: Matthew's dad

CHAPTER 6 – LEARNING

1. Read at least 50 books a year – ideally batched in one or more short bursts of intense reading. Hat Tip: Bill Gates
2. Manically take notes – with a pen and paper. If you want to look cool and create opportunities for future serendipity, use a Moleskine and go back through it periodically. See: *The Benefits of Writing With Good Old Fashioned Pen And Paper (Huff Post)* by Catherine Pearson
3. Walk regularly; ensuring you mediate, read or listen to audiobooks. See: *In Praise of Walking - The new science of how we walk and why it's good for us* by Shane O'Mara
4. Tiago Forte's digital system for systematically synthesising past ideas, inspirations, and insights
5. Understand the difference in learning modes. See: *Mastering the Rockefeller Habits* by Verne Harnish
6. Find what enables you to find flow (e.g. music). See: *Flow* by Mihaly Csikszentmihalyi
7. Build your anti-library. Hat tip: the Japanese concept of 'Tsundoku' – being the acquiring of reading materials and letting them pile up without reading them
8. Use story, or vision, boards. Hat tip: author Emma Mactaggart
9. Flip it; that is invert, always invert. Hat tip: Carl Jacobi
10. Collect your favourite quotes. Hat tip: Winston Churchill: "It is a good thing for an uneducated man to read books of quotations."

CHAPTER 7 – PRINCIPLES

1. Barry Schwartz's Paradox of Choice – More is less; too much choice creates diminished benefits
2. Parkinson's Law – Tasks expand to fill available time
3. Pareto Principle – 80% of outcomes are due to 20% of the inputs

4. Peter Principle – When someone is promoted to the level of incompetence.
5. Paul Principle – When someone is promoted out of the position in which they can do the most damage
6. Bloch's Axiom – You will spend longer looking for something than the time it would have taken to simply recreate it
7. Cohn's Law – Bureaucracy is about paperwork increasing evermore; with ever less actual work. Stability arrives when 100% of resources are spent reporting on absolutely nothing
8. Anderson's Axiom – You can only be young once; but you can be immature forever
9. Nassim Taleb's Skin in the Game – Having a measurable risk when taking a major decision is necessary for fairness
10. Believe in the Butterfly Effect – A small change in one state of deterministic nonlinear systems can result in large differences at a later stage

CHAPTER 8 – TECH

1. Religiously use folders in your email inbox and have the discipline to check them every month. See: *Getting Things Done* by David Allen
2. Listen to audiobooks (including podcasts) on at least double speed, even up to 3 or 3.5 speed. See: *Can we speed-listen and still understand?* by Matt Inouye
3. Dictate everything. See: *How Dictation Benefits Cognitive Productivity* by Luc P. Beaudoin
4. Turn off all notifications including sound on all devices and turn on greyscale for your smart devices. See: *The One Thing* by Gary Keller and Jay Papasan
5. Actively look to habit iterate; for example, replace social media hits by reading a chapter of a book. See: *The Power of Habit* by Charles Duhigg
6. Peter Diamandis' 6Ds:
    a. Digitisation
    b. Disruption
    c. Dematerialise (from physical to digital)
    d. Demonetisation – i.e. the dropping of price
    e. Democratisation – access for all
    f. Deceptive – at first there seems to be no growth

7. Fast, frictionless, fun and free. See: *Frictionless: Why the Future of Everything Will Be Fast, Fluid, and Made Just for You* by Christiane Lemieux
8. Print it. See: *Reader, Come Home: The Reading Brain in a Digital World* by Maryanne Wolf
9. Upwork. Fiverr. Airtasker. See: *How To be a Productivity Ninja* by Graham Allcott
10. Make everything as simple as possible; however no simpler. Hat tip: Albert Einstein

CHAPTER 9 – FRAMEWORKS

1. Why is it not WD 39? See: *The Art of Innovation: Lessons in Creativity* from Ideo, America's Leading Design Firm by Tom Kelley
2. The meaning of life is meaning. See: *Man's Search for Meaning* by Viktor Frankl
3. Common sense; is uncommon. See: *Uncommon Sense, Common Nonsense: Why some organisations consistently outperform others* by Jules Goddard and Tony Eccles
4. Silence is golden. You have two ears and one mouth. Use them in those proportions. Hat tip: Epictetus
5. Write your Life Handbook (this is ours). See: *The Seven-Day Weekend* by Ricardo Semler
6. Have a BHAV (Big Hairy Audacious Vision). Hat tip: Jim Collins
7. Planning is more important than the activity. Hat tip: Abraham Lincoln: "If I had 8 hours to chop down a tree, I would spend 6 of those hours sharpening my axe."
8. Walk into the room of mirrors. Hat tip: Roy & HG and see: *The Slight Edge: Turning Simple Disciplines into Massive Success and Happiness* by Jeff Olson and John David Mann
9. Get back up one more time than the next person – move from failure to failure without the loss of enthusiasm. See: *Our Iceberg is Melting* by John Kotter
10. It is the journey not the destination. Hat tip: Ralph Waldo Emerson

CHAPTER 10 – TIPS

1. Understand that it is normally at least 10 years to become an overnight success. See: *Talent Is Never Enough* by John C. Maxwell
2. Excellence comes from being uncomfortable. See: *A Beautiful Constraint: How to Transform Your Limitations Into Advantages, and Why It's Everyone's Business* by Adam Morgan and Mark Barden

3. If you want what the 1% have, you need to do what 99% won't. See: *Born Standing Up* by Steve Martin
4. Charlie Munger's 25 Tendencies of Human Misjudgement. See: *Poor Charlie's Almanack* by Charlie Munger
5. Live like you will die tomorrow. Learn like you will live forever. Hat tip: Mahatma Gandhi
6. To begin with success, start at the end. See: *Chop Wood Carry Water* by Joshua Medcalf
7. Be prepared. Hat tip: founder of the Scouts movement, Robert Baden-Powell
8. Aim for the stars. Hat tip: Mary Poppins
9. Reverse psychology is a thing. See: *Super Thinking: The Big Book of Mental Models* by Gabriel Weinberg and Lauren McCann
10. Less. Is. More. See: *Essentialism: The Disciplined Pursuit of Less* by Greg McKeown

Acknowledgements

This book is the result of contributions from a number of people, each of whom we thank. In particular:

(1) The team we work with at View Legal.
(2) All members of the View adviser community inspire us to do better each day.
(3) Finally, thank you to our family, for being on this journey with us.

Interested to learn more?

1. Subscribe to the free weekly blog posts:

http://blog.viewlegal.com.au/?m=1

To subscribe to the blog, simply enter your email address in the subscription box in the right hand column or alternatively, subscribe through your preferred RSS feed from your browser.

2. View Communities

The View Communities membership platform provides you with significant access to our community discussion group, free access to our webinars, workshops and roadshows, unlimited access to many of our ebooks, and mentoring sessions with specialist View lawyers.

Learn more at—

https://comviewnities.com/

3. Education programs

View Legal specialises in all forms of adviser education and collaborative learning.

We are fortunate to regularly present to accountants, financial planners, other lawyers and risk advisers.

Our programs are tailored to meet your specific requirements and can be delivered in lengths ranging from 20 minute web-based updates to 5 day in-house courses (and every permutation in between) and formats including in person, webinar and video streaming. Our most popular sessions tend to be 90 minute team trainings, which can be recorded for future use.

A sample of some of our current topics is set out at the following link—

http://viewlegal.com.au/product-category/events/

You can also explore and enroll to all of our View University courses at this link—

https://viewuni.com/

More generally, each View University course is designed to be relevant for all advisers including accountants, financial advisers and lawyers, other than lawyers who have specialised in the trusts and estate planning space for many years.

With 35 discrete learning modules and over 15 hours of technical content in each course, including webinars, vidcasts, and technical papers, the university level courses are the first of their kind in the Australian marketplace.

To learn more about each course and View University more generally, see—

> https://viewuni.com/.

4. Business model iteration

Matthew Burgess has been recognised as a thought leader in delivery of professional service solutions by peers, industry commentators and competitors. He regularly presents keynotes in this area as well as coordinating and facilitating firm retreats and education programs.

Indeed, Matthew is the only practising lawyer in Australia who is a Certified Speaking Professional (CSP), a designation conferred by the Professional Speakers Australia (PSA), the industry's leading organisation. The CSP is likewise the speaking profession's international measure of professional platform competence.

Matthew is counted among the rare 12 percent of professional speakers worldwide who currently hold the CSP credential.

Learn more about Matthew's business model presentations here—

> https://viewlegal.com.au/matthewburgessspeaking/

Learn more about the 3 business books Matthew has written—

> http://www.thedreamenabler.com.au/

Other Reading

A Selection of Other Books from View Legal

For all the latest books please visit *https://viewlegal.com.au/books/*

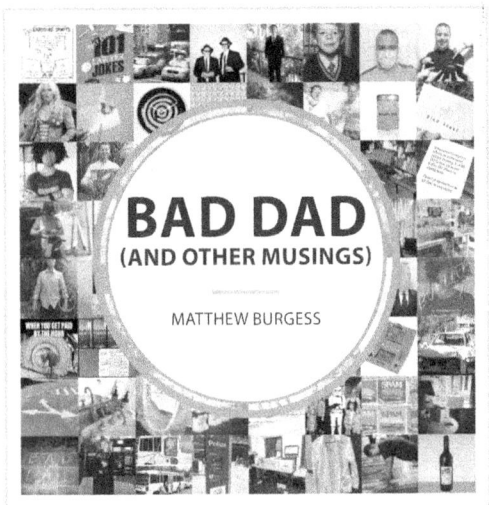

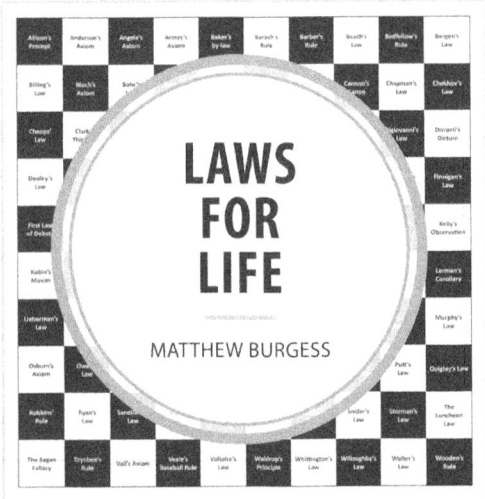

About

About View

At View Legal our mantra is to be 'for friends'.

In other words, creating solutions and value propositions that are compelling to our friends.

To achieve our vision, we have set out to fundamentally and radically revolutionise access to high quality legal advice, in our areas of deep specialisation – structuring, tax, trusts, asset protection, business sales, estate and succession planning.

To help explain the approach View is taking to uniquely deliver valuable legal solutions, the following table lists 10 traditional ways law firms have operated (and, almost exclusively, continue to operate) and the new vision that View is built around.

Old view	View Legal
Bill clients on hourly rates (or various, increasingly elaborate, permutations on the theme) and have no particular interest in client perception of value	Customers provided up front 'SPS Guarantee' – that is service and price satisfaction is guaranteed with all work undertaken following upfront fixed pricing
Everything tracked on a timesheet. The longer something takes, the better	No timesheets. Sophisticated project management tools used to help ensure customer expectations are exceeded
Quality is defined by the law firm	Quality is defined by the customer
'Impressive' CBD office space, with 'dominant' fit outs	View meets where best suits customers. No permanent CBD space retained
Intellectual property is how we make money and should be guarded jealously	Intellectual property is how we create trust and should be shared freely
Lawyers striving to deliver near-perfect technical excellence	All service designed to be fit-for-purpose, aligning with collaboratively agreed customer objectives
Lawyers cultural focus on 'is this billable' for the firm	Lawyers cultural focus on 'is this valuable' for the customer
'Leveraging' of full-time lawyers to do the bulk of the work serving clients	Flexible work practices that match supply with demand
Constant focus on the 'need for diversity' of gender	Only focus on diversity of thought
Revenue growth the #1 goal	Exceeding customer expectations #1 goal

Significant inspiration provided by VeraSage. Partly adapted with permission of George Beaton, Beaton Capital.

If you would like to learn more about any of the above solutions or View more generally contact, email solutions@viewlegal.com.au.

About the Authors

Matthew Burgess is one of the founders of specialist firm View Legal.

Having the opportunity to help clients achieve their goals is what he is most passionate about.

As Matthew always works in conjunction with trusted advisers (whether it be accountants, financial advisers or other lawyers) and their clients, finding ways to fundamentally improve the value received by those advisers, and in turn their clients, has led him to develop numerous game changing models. Examples include providing guaranteed upfront fixed pricing, founding what is widely regarded as Australia's first virtual law firm, and more recently, developing a platform that gives advisers access to market leading advice and support for less than $10 a week.

Matthew's specialisation in tax, structuring, asset protection, estate and succession planning has seen him recognised by most leading industry associations including the Tax Institute, the Weekly Tax Bulletin and in the 2014 'Best Lawyers' list for trusts and estates and either personally, or as part of View, since 2015 in 'Doyles' for taxation and since 2017 for wills, estates and succession planning.

Work is one aspect of his life Matthew loves, so there is no need to be constantly searching for 'balance'. His other great loves are:

1. Family – they are profiled in various ways through the series of children's books he has written under the pseudonym 'Lily Burgess' – see *www.wordsfromdaddysmouth.com.au* and various TV commercials;
2. Learning – going cold-turkey on television and most forms of media in late 2005 has radically increased Matthew's ability to study the great authors and inspired him to publish a series of books that explore the concept of 'true success' – see *www.the-dreamenabler.com.au*
3. Health – aside from being a foodie and swimming at least 5kms a week, Matthew installed a stand up workstation in 2007 and among a few other lifestyle choices, it changed his life.

Dyan Burgess is passionate about helping entrepreneurs select, organise and take care of their diverse, accomplished and valuable experiences into a compelling, multi-platform, independently published book.

In her work as Creative Director for 'Words From Daddy's Mouth', she knows first-hand what it is like to pull the best bits of many and varied experiences into unique and passionate stories.

As a country girl beginning life in rural Victoria and NSW, you can probably imagine the gorgeous surrounds, quirky people and outdoor adventures that dotted the landscape of her early years. A fascination with people and their vast potential followed her through a science degree in Brisbane, Australia, extending into two decades of banking and finance, travel adventures, family creation and business development.

Beginning in the independent publishing industry can be daunting. Coming to understand the multiple facets of the publishing industry has been incredibly fascinating to Dyan. However, as a writer (and entrepreneur), these aspects can seem redundant (and boring) - and this can stop writers from achieving publication of a book. Dyan has always enjoyed collaborating to realise writer's (and entrepreneur's) dreams. So whether you are interested in the technical aspects of publishing, or you simply want to write a book on your expertise, she can point you in the correct direction.

Simply put – Getting it Done.

Behind the Scenes

"Outtakes" from the process of making this book...

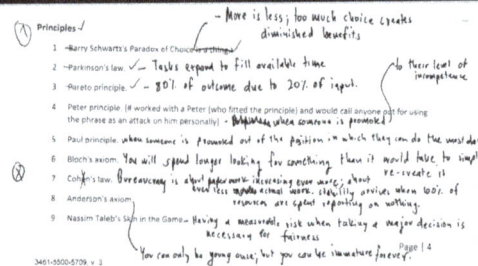

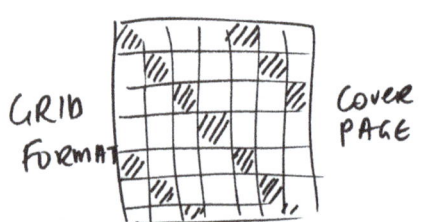

50. 100% v 99%
51. chocke points
52. honour absent
53. KISS
54. 4eye
55. and not or
56. coin toss
57. Paul's Principle (cold enough to chance out of leverage)
58. Bloch's Axiom (ueway) (position) chilbs
59. Cohn's Law
60. Music
61. Dropbox
62. OCR
63. Anderson's Axiom
64. green smoothie
65. Great shoes + bed (+ spouse)
66. Humour
67. Have Hero's
68. Story telling
69. Anti-library
70. 6 pillars of self esteem (moleskin summary)
71. 9 criteria (moleskin - Sharma)
72. Bucketlist
73. Uberify

74. reverse mentoring (cups less full)
75. 8th wonder compounding
76. 10 yrs = overnight
77. Steal (don't borrow)
78. Democritisation
79. live like a stoic
80. Walking adventures
81. Allow serendipity
82. foster sycronicity
83. strategy; not plans (SLB find?)
84. WD40
85. greatest strength; greatest weakness
86. Breath
87. Skin in game
88. uncomfortable
89. meaning of life; meaning
90. point of wealth; earn it yourself
91. Viral on S.Media test
92. Butterfly effect
93. Goldilocks principle
94. Silence 2 ears 1 mouth
95. Next step

96. early to bed (early to rise, work hard & exercise)
97. write life handbook
98. BHAG
99. Ship
100. P.S.A.
101. one full day off i family
102. regular breaks
103. Hobbie around goal's -eg family hobbies
104. gratitude letters
105. posture
106. vocal strength
107. Story board
108. planning as important as activity
109. Room of mirrors
110. A measure = impact you have on others
111. checklists
112. flip it
113. 10 minutes early, 10/al
114. collect quotes
115. journey not destination
116. Fast, Frictionless, Free

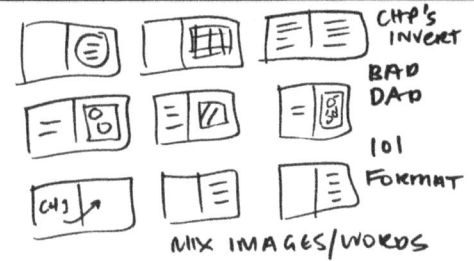

Eva Lotta Lamm — Building People

'BOOKS ARE MADE OUT OF BOOKS'
— CORMAC MCCARTHY

Austin Kleon
Show Yr Work

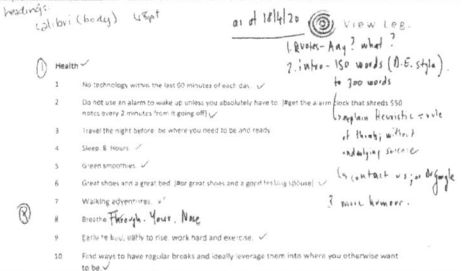

www.ingramcontent.com/pod-product-compliance
Lightning Source LLC
Chambersburg PA
CBHW080612300426
43661CB00144B/908